Spotlight on the

Art of

I0022313

Leadership

Edited By:

Rebecca Fegan

Contributors:

Janel Asche ▪ Mark Fegan

Rebecca Fegan ▪ Pamela Hughes ▪ Christine Jones

Keith Jones ▪ Randy Prier

Spotlight on the Art of Leadership

Contributors:

Janel Asche, Mark Fegan, Rebecca Fegan, Pamela Hughes, Christine Jones, Keith Jones, Randy Prier

Copyright © 2025 Alternative Book Club.

All rights reserved.

Published by Keith Jones / Kitewind LLC

ISBN **978-1-964649-02-3**

Edited by Rebecca Fegan

Cover Design by Keith Jones, alternativebookclub.com.

Printed and bound in the United States of America.

First Edition

All rights reserved. No part of the material protected by this copyright notice may be reproduced or utilized in any form or by any means, electronic or mechanical, including photocopying, recording or by any information storage or retrieval system without the written permission of the copyright owner.

Preface

John C. Maxwell, Leadership guru and author of at least 100 books said, "He who thinks he is leading and has no one following, is only taking a walk in the park."

Often as I stroll "down the road" leading my group or project, I find myself turning around to see if I am only taking a walk. How did I end up in a leadership position?

I used to think that leading meant being in front and pointing the way, giving orders, directing traffic. So, if my group was going to learn and grow, they had to get their information and skills only from me and my co-leader. We had to tell them what to do all the time. So…that was a rough two months. They were bored, we were scrambling, and there was dissention in the ranks. What I believed was the function of leadership was the complete opposite of what we discovered while working with this group! Lynn and I completely changed our approach to leading the group and, as a result, four of the group achieved recognition and awards five years later.

Since then, I've had to grow in character, knowledge, and skill to fill the shoes of a leader.

So many books on leadership will list the character qualities and values you have to have, the knowledge and skills you have to develop, the connections you need to make, but having a check-off list completed doesn't finish the job.

This is **not** a "how-to" book on leadership. Everyone starts from a different place—physically, mentally, and spiritually, and there are as many paths to leadership as there are people. In this book, several different writers describe aspects of their own personal leadership experiences and how those experiences impacted them. Now, necessarily, in such an effort, you might pick up some insights that could be helpful to you in your own leadership opportunities--things to either emulate or avoid. But these writers make no claim to be perfect or even highly accomplished leaders. It is simply that throughout their careers, for whatever reason, they have often found themselves in positions of leadership. Some they sought, others sought them. Don't be misled, they're as ambitious as anyone else. It's just that landing in a leadership position isn't always the result of purposeful effort.

You don't read a leadership book, tick off the boxes, then look for something you can lead. Watch a flock of starlings. They aren't following one bird. They are swooping and soaring and diving as a group and never run into each other. Yet you have no idea where they're going to be at a particular moment of time and which bird will be leading. It is similar to the leadership paths people follow.

1. There are opportunities to lead that come up because a group needs a volunteer.
2. There are pet projects you want to finish that people want to help you with because they align with their ideals.
3. There are offices you wish to fill because it is something you're wanting to contribute to the group, and you apply, make your case, and get elected.
4. And to be honest, there are times when you just fall into the leadership role.

What we intend to do with this book is to make you more aware of leadership issues you will face, because, like it or not, you will probably end up in a leadership role of some sort. You will see how each of us found ourselves in leadership roles, the lessons we learned, the awareness we've gained, the resources we discovered...and you may recognize yourself in these pages. You will forge your own path through leadership, of course, but we would encourage you to keep a leadership journal so your "notes to self" collection all ends up in the same place—where you can find it!

Spotlight on the Art of Leadership
Contents

1

Notes to Self

By: Rebecca Fegan

"Leadership is Influence—no more, no less"
~John C. Maxwell

Notes to Self, My Discoveries

Leadership: What is it? Many books will start out with a definition from the dictionary. I, however, am just going to tell you what my **perception** of leadership is. The definitions are so vague that thousands of books are written to clear it up. There are countless motivational speakers and businessmen that go from venue to venue, from company event to company event to "Show people the Way" to fill those leadership shoes. But if these truly worked, there'd be no more call for these types of events, yet there are more and more every day.

Many folks find themselves in leadership positions and having to muddle through somehow. They are among those who have leadership thrust onto them. I was one of those. I never considered myself a leader. I was content to just do what needed to be done without a committee or oversight. I would rather work by myself than work with a group. Leadership seemed like doing everything to make sure someone else got the work done and not getting your hands dirty. I thought it was cheating.

Giving orders and looking over someone's shoulder didn't look like the kind of thing I EVER wanted to do. But because I am a curious person, I noted good and bad approaches to leadership should I ever have to assume the role...never believing for one second that I'd have to. I did start making discoveries, and it occurred to me that if I kept track of them, I wouldn't have to rediscover them over and over.

I started writing *Notes to Self* in various and sundry places so I could remember the lessons I learned while I was observing leadership and when I was in leadership positions later. There were notes on my phone, notes on napkins, in book margins, on scraps of paper, and receipts in my purse. I was cleaning out a notebook and found a couple of real gems that I could have used if I'd remembered I'd written them. I resolved to keep all these *Notes to self* in a binder. I also wrote the back story of those notes: what I was doing, who was in the group, what part I played, etc.

Perceptions

Based on these notes, I discovered some perceptions I had about leadership and the revelations I received when those assumptions were way off base. For instance: I concluded that only pretty or popular people lead. I was neither. I was never the captain of pick-up baseball or kickball teams. I was never the captain of the academic team. In group projects (I **hate** group projects!) I was the one that did the lion's share of the work while the leader would do minimal work and get all the credit. We played as a group, we won or lost as a group, and, in school, we were graded as a group, so if I wanted a good grade, I either had to either **do** all the work or **edit** all the work. I know I'm not the only person with this experience.

I remember the time when the leader of my group assigned me a part of the project, and instead of doing everyone's work, all I did was my own. I refused to help the other members of the group. Because the leader was afraid that I'd embarrass the other members of the team because their contributions were shallow, short, and inconsequential, he arranged a preemptive retaliation against me for the final grade by presenting all the other contributors' work. While speaking in glowing terms about how everyone came together to make this project a success. *He didn't present my part of the project at all and told the teacher I wasn't a team player.* I showed the teacher that I had done my work and had been prepared to present it, and though he gave my work an

A, he still flunked me on the group project. The teacher suggested that my biggest contribution to the team should not be my expertise in researching, writing, and presenting my part of the assignment, but in working as a group to improve the group project.

> *Note to Self:* Leadership is facilitating cooperation in the team. Though it *may seem* goal-oriented, the end product is not the purpose of the team--it's cooperating and working together to gain a synergy that makes the end product more than the sum of its parts. I was quite bitter when I wrote this.

This *Note to Self* seemed ridiculous at first glance. What's the point of getting a team together if the goal isn't to solve the problem or do the project? But when you look at the deeper purpose, you get an inkling. Aha! The purpose of the team is not to solve <u>a specific problem</u>!

> *Restated Note to Self:* You should be developing an "A Team" that becomes the go-to group on anything important. *If you have a good crew, they can solve ALL the problems and successfully complete ALL of the projects assigned to them regardless of the challenges.*

How did my incorrect perception affect the group?

I was not a popular person to have on a team. When I was assigned to a team, the reaction of the team was a collective sigh of resignation. It was the sound that the group made when they had to take the nerd in the pick-up baseball team. (Oh NO! not Timmy! When you tell him to run home, he heads for his house!) I can count on one hand the number of times I got chosen for a team; I was usually assigned.

My mistaken assumption of the nature of leadership affected my perception of the group project and my place in it. If I had a bad attitude, it didn't matter what the quality of my work was. If I was condescending to the members of the group, they wouldn't try. The leader would be threatened and uncooperative, and, most importantly, *the team wouldn't gel!* If the team didn't gel, assignments would consist of last-minute research, bad or missing analysis, horrible writing with typos, misspellings, grammar issues, and apathetic performance on the whole.

My biggest perception change was this: A leader is one who grows the group and molds it into an organism that works and thinks together to do projects or solve problems. As a participant, I should support the leader and attempt to keep the morale of the group high enough that people are excited to be part of it.

My first '*Notes to self*' looked like this:

- A leader grows the group and molds it into an organism that works and thinks together to do projects or solve problems.

- Ask, Don't tell! Questions make your teammates see that you value their input and their intuition. They may surprise you with their insight, creativity, and resourcefulness!

- Seek to bolster morale. Support and praise go a long way to helping a team develop rapport and think together, make use of their strengths, and improve the quality of their work.

- Knowledge of the people is better than knowledge of the work.

All of these "**Notes to Self**" come at a price, often painful. Missteps, autocratic rule, and low morale is bad enough in the workplace, but deadly in volunteer organizations! My change in perception and attitude resulted in a much-improved performance in the groups I was involved in. There was a feeling of pride and accomplishment that, until I understood that changing myself was my first priority, I found elusive. The more I grew my thinking, the better we worked together. You could tell! The team members got benefits and value from the group. Let me tell you the story of those discoveries.

What did I need to change?

At one point in my life, I entered the fast food universe. I was put into a training program to learn to be a manager. I went through all the positions in the restaurant, watching videos, studying the menu items, and practicing my skills in a burger joint across the street from the VA hospital. It was a valuable experience for several reasons:

1. It was a 24-hour store, so I worked each of the shifts at one point or another.
2. The crew had been working in this training store for a long time (which in fast food is anything over six weeks).
3. It was a $1,000,000 store with a very experienced manager.
4. We were dealing with military families, nursing staff, and neighborhood families so we were consistently busy learning to serve food in a friendly manner, and yet keep the premises clean and inviting.

It was quite a challenge! I was a newly minted graduate with a business management degree, and I was well-versed in just-in-time inventory, labor/management relations, statistics, and accounting. All that education was for naught in my position as an associate manager I tried to make the processes more efficient and, at the same time, follow the instructions of the other associate managers and general manager. In doing exactly as I had been taught; everything was correct but took twice as long when I was there. I didn't trust the intuition of the crew because my education in management discouraged that type of thinking! Slow and perfect is not preferable in a *FAST* food restaurant. I was told I was not a good fit and fired. I was very disappointed.

> *Note to Self:* Knowledge of the people is better than knowledge of the work. Knowing all the technical aspects of a job does not make you better at leading the people in it.

I cried all the way home and considered myself a failure. My friend, Dave, had pity on me and hired me on as a crewmember at the branch of the same restaurant in the town where we lived. After a while, he asked me to be crew chief. It was more money, so I took it. I was older so I didn't have to adhere to a school schedule, and he put me on the morning shift. Most of the people I worked with were my age or older. As a crew chief, I really didn't have to do much with this group. They were "self-managed" and knew how to anticipate the needs of the production line just by intuition and experience. They weren't looking at timelines and charts and graphs. There was a certain rhythm we got into during the rush hour and though we were calling production (how many of which kind of meat to put on the grill, the number of each type of hamburgers, fries, and fish or chicken to cook), it was like a ballet.

I had the misfortune of living a half-block from the restaurant, so if they were short on a shift or running into problems, they would call me, and I'd show up. Any time that I was called in to work night crew, they were already in a panic because they "thought they could handle it." These crewmen were not incompetent. They were good, but they didn't work like a team. They'd be short a few crewmen, overwhelmed by a couple of football busses, and ankle-high in lettuce when I walked in. By the time we closed the doors, the product was restocked, the grill clean, the oil filtered, the oven ready for breakfast biscuits, and the floor was spotless.

The night crew was made up of teenagers still in school or newly graduated. To get things done, I had to take a different approach than I had at the training store. Instead of giving orders, I was asking for help. "I'll get the grill clean if you restock the hamburger patties and fries. What do you want to clean next? Whatever you hate to clean, I'll do that."

We told jokes. We played a game where you had to name a song that started with the last letter of the previous answer. "Yesterday." "Yellow Rose of Texas." "Sweet Caroline." Then everyone would add "Ba Ba Baaaaaaa…" I showed them what working on a good team looked like.

We moved some of the night crew to the weekend daytime shift. They saw how we worked with much lower stress. They started showing more respect for the day crew, and the day crew enjoyed working with the night crew because they knew how to have fun.

Note to Self: Ask, don't tell.

Note to Self: Pay attention to morale. Less-stressed people do better work.

How did I go about changing my perception?

Most of my leadership training didn't come from a book or a manual. I observed good leaders. Then I discovered what leading was NOT.

Our store was designated as a training store in my second year there. We had the highest food safety and health inspection scores of the franchise, the lowest turn-over, and the fewest complaints. We were chosen to train managers for new restaurants.

Bob was the owner of the newest restaurant which was being built near the interstate. He was great to work with. He knew what questions to ask, and he put his back into all the training. He was fantastic on the "front line" where the orders were taken, and money exchanged hands. He had a great rapport with all the customers, and he wasn't bad on the backline where all the cooking and assembly was done. But his associate managers (we called them Bert and Ernie) were obnoxious!

Let me introduce you to the hierarchy of fast-food restaurants.

- The General Manager or GM runs the store, and he is assisted by two to four assistant managers.
- The frontline supervisor works with those who have direct contact with the customers.
- The backline supervisor works with those who have direct contact with the food.
- The #1 sandwich maker does the large sandwiches that take lots of prep
- The #2 sandwich maker does the small sandwiches and the specialty sandwiches such as fish, chicken, ham and cheese, or roast beef.

The #1 and #2 sandwich makers basically run the cooking part of the store, so the backline supervisor is usually the #1 sandwich maker. I was the #1 sandwich maker and Mikey was #2, but since we were training Bert and Ernie, Bert was standing in for the #1 sandwich position. Mikey was one of the fastest sandwich makers in the store and you could count on one hand how many mistakes he made in a month. Bert immediately started to treat Mikey with disdain. Big mistake!

Bert's philosophy was, "My way or the highway. He kept saying, "Mikey has to learn to respect the shirt." (Managers got button up cotton shirts while the crew wore the company polo shirts.) At one point he threw a wad of paper at him to get his attention, and Mikey almost walked out. I said to this arrogant manager, sotto voce, "Bert? Just tell him what you need." He replied, "I have to get his attention first. He's got the attention span of a gnat." Like I said: he was obnoxious.

Bert didn't understand the people he worked with, and he was not very competent at the work. So, he made up in bluster and bombastic speech for what he didn't know about leadership. We got very far behind in filling orders. Timers were going off due to wait-times missed at the window and the counter. There were over ten orders on the order screen. The crew was waiting for Bert to tell them what to do, and he hadn't a clue. After about minutes of this, I kicked him off the line and told him to start stocking the coolers. He was incensed.

In the briefing after the rush, Bernie blamed everything on his crew and me. He was especially upset that I had embarrassed him in front of the crew and had raised my voice to him. He recommended I be fired. I hadn't seen my General Manager mad before. He was livid.

Ernie, on the other hand, was always looking for a way to get out of work, so he didn't do well on the back line at all, and on the front line, the customers actually groaned when they saw him on the cash register. We warned Bob that his Associate Managers were not going to last very long.

Bert and Ernie did finally graduate from our store, but they had nothing nice to say about us. Bob was extremely disappointed in their performance at his store in Rockport. He told us that at one point, the two had a fistfight <u>on the front line in full view of customers</u>. He fired them on the spot. We sent a couple of our people to help him out, but it was a thirty-mile commute.

Bert and Ernie had ignored the ideas:
1. Ask, Don't Tell
2. Knowledge of the people is better than knowledge of the work
3. High morale is sacrificed when abusive language is used

This was the point where I started keeping my "Notes to Self" in a binder.

SPOTLIGHT ON THE ART OF LEADERSHIP

My new perception of leadership

Looking at how my perception of leadership changed, *instead of building a team that could solve one problem, we had a crew that could handle anything.* One year, we handled the Great Snowstorm that knocked out all the power in the neighborhoods, so we were the only source of food in a 20-block area and working with 50%-75% of our crew due to snow hazards. We handled 2 robberies in three years. We handled a gang war in our parking lot one spring after a prom went bad. We handled 4 temporary managers because the general manager quit and then handled a store full of customers during a tornado another year. All in all, it was an exciting five years of experience!

One thing I noticed in all the jobs and volunteer work in my experience was that unless the crews worked together, the atmosphere became confrontational.

Regardless of the situation, there are Day Crew-Night Crew wars, Sales-Management wars, and even Offense-Defense wars. Each group within any organization has certain temperamental traits that make them a good team. Those traits are often at loggerheads with the other groups, (even if they're on the same team!) because of the demands of the jobs they do.

To illustrate these concepts, I use sports examples because you can easily see the correspondence to other types of teams--either corporate or community. What makes defensive teams in sports successful enough to use brute force to stop the opposing team from scoring? <u>Reactionary</u> awareness. The plotting and strategic/tactical thinking of the offensive team focuses on the mental acuity to <u>respond</u> to defensive actions rather than to <u>react</u>. In the locker room or on the practice field, though, animosity can build up. Each side strives to use the strengths of the opposition to their disadvantage. In other words, it's like Jiu Jitsu. The smaller, weaker opponent uses the strength and power of their opponent against them. If the big guy runs at the little guy, the little guy steps aside and adds a kick or push so the big guy cannot stop, and his attacker converts his strength from a weapon to a way of avoiding a tree.

The offensive team may be condescending to the defense because they consider them less intelligent. Why? Because the offensive team practices plays in an attempt to outsmart their opponents to gain yardage or make goals. They have practiced *responding.* The defensive team may look at how badly the offensive team protects their quarterback or provides coverage for the shooter in basketball or soccer, and think of the offense as weak and ineffective because the defense has practiced *reacting*. They start sniping at each other and their morale drops. Should the team, as a whole, lose several games in a row, each side would blame the other for ineffective play.

Developing my compass

How do we avoid that kind of conflict? There are many qualities, values, and character traits that the leader has to have to work with the Jekyll and Hyde aspects of a team. The most difficult quality I had to develop was my *empathy*. There is a very specific boundary between management and crew, between teacher and student, and between coach and participant. Empathy is essential to understanding the people you work with. But as a leader, you cannot care more about the growth of your people than they do.

This was the situation:

My oldest daughter was in third grade, and it was time to move from Daisy Scouts to Brownies. The District Council scheduled a meeting with the parents to determine how to organize this brownie troop. They needed troop leaders to volunteer so the district could see to their training and understanding issues such as dues, legal responsibilities, the curriculum, the requirements for advancement, cookie sales... You get the idea.

I was one of two parents that showed up. This did not bode well. I had never been a Girl Scout. Lynn, my soon-to-be best friend, had been a leader, but since she worked an 8-hour shift at the local grocery store, she didn't think she could devote enough time to being a leader again. However, she did say she would be a Co-leader if I took on this responsibility. I sighed. We went through the required training and had our first meeting.

This is how we began our leadership journey:

We started out with thirteen little girls. We planned which programs and badges we thought we could achieve that year without any input from the girls.

(This was before I'd started my folder for *Notes to Self.* We started without the approach to leadership…Ask, Don't Tell.)

By the second month, we had lost complete control. We talked on the phone and came up with this gem: Why should we care more about the growth of these girls than they do? Well? What do they care about? We listed a bunch of things that we thought little girls in third grade cared about. Then it occurred to us to ASK THE GIRLS! So, we had another meeting and changed our approach.

We discovered they wanted to be an outside troop! (Who knew?!) and they wanted badges for things like camping, hiking, and cooking. Then we invited the moms of these little girls to talk about what they do, their jobs, their responsibilities, what they did for fun, and, interestingly enough, the things they wanted to change about their lives. We sent a letter home with each girl with the questions and a schedule of our meetings. In being empathetic, the girls were exposed to a different type of leadership than they had at home or school. They had control, They had their own goals. They had a voice. With the empathy that Lynn and I developed, the girls took on more of the responsibilities because it was their plan! We were right there with them, supporting them and encouraging them.

It was Fascinating! Who would have imagined that nine-year-old girls would want to have that kind of determination in activities and goals for themselves and the group as a whole?

There were two troops in our little town: our group—the outside troop, and one other—the inside troop. Over the years our troop was together, from third grade to seventh grade we had many activities:

- We went tent-camping.
- We spent a week at the Girl Scout Camp in Nebraska City where we worked on making kites, cooking, and doing the high elements of the ropes course.
- We spent a weekend at Indian Cave State Park.
- We went on "high adventure" activities with some other troops: Camping in the Snow, Orienteering, CPR/First Aid, and a two-day canoe trip!

- We went to Worlds of Fun in Kansas City and saw the Nelson Art Gallery and the Doll Museum as well.
- We had fundraisers in addition to cookie sales.
- We even went on an archaeological dig in South Dakota where we dug up beads and pottery at an actual site!

But the most exciting activity was our Junior Trip to Rocky Mountain National Park. It was so inspiring that one of the girls decided she wanted to be either a park ranger or get a degree in physical education and recreation and work at one of the parks. (She worked at this very park for two years before heading off to college.)

They got their hiking badge, camping badge, backpacking badge, and horse riding badge! They explored the climbing wall, went swimming, and saw their first mountains (entering through Estes Park, gripping the armrests, and trying not to look down the side of the mountain) and their first waterfall. They got caught in a rainstorm *with hail* on the side of a mountain and packed up three tents, all the cooking pots and pans, the sleeping bags, and their clothes, and left the campsite as if no one had ever been there…in fifteen minutes! They ran nearly 3 miles back to the parking lot! All the girls in the troop got their Girl Scout Silver awards.

The Inside Troop, where my youngest daughter, Jo, belonged, had their junior trip in a local hotel and did each other's hair and nails. That trip culminated in a fashion show of sorts. Jo was terribly disappointed. No one but the leader's daughter got a silver award in that troop.

I think I collected about eight *Notes to Self* just on this trip. I found those when I was cleaning out my backpack for a family vacation and added them to my folder. Here are some of them:

Note to Self: Pack for every type of weather

Note to Self: Make sure everyone knows how to set up their tents before leaving on the trip.

Note to Self: Make plans on how to handle homesickness with the girls early.

Note to Self: Carry extra small notebooks for people to journal in. (Staves off homesickness!)

Note to Self: Buy postcards at every destination to send home to families during the trip.

Now most of those don't seem to apply to leadership, but they speak to thinking ahead, handling interpersonal relationships among the members of the team, and getting buy-in and cooperation from the group.

I used nearly all of those notes (except for the tent set-up) as a band parent. I discovered that what those had in common was the quality of *empathy*. This quality was essential for those moments when members needed support and understanding.

But it also helped when requesting help from members to remember what their pain points were. We don't ask them to walk a mile in someone's shoes and then stomp on their feet. I had to learn how to couch my requests in a way that would serve the person as well as the group. If I knew Julie liked attention and rewards, I would publicly praise her or give her a certificate. If I knew Emily wanted an exchange of value, I'd offer to do a chore for her if she'd do one for me. (She was exceptional in art, so she would design our t-shirts and our posters for events, In return, I'd be in charge of the cleanup for her assigned meeting. They all took turns cleaning up after the meetings.

The main problem I had was a little girl named Brittany (No, it's not her real name.) She had more problems at home than I could deal with. We'd make some progress, and she'd be cooperative for a little while, then she'd make some outrageous demand, or refuse to do her part, or have a temper tantrum. Empathy was not enough to work that out.

I learned **patience** when, during the cookie sale, Brittany's brother found all the money she'd collected and spent it on candy. When we tried to collect the money, we ended up having to go through the legal department. Brittany's mom wasn't going to pay since she didn't think that the actions of her son were her fault.

I learned **perseverance** when we went to the archaeological dig and Brittany decided she didn't have to help in the dig when it was her turn to take the dirt we'd excavated needed to be sifted. She would quit the minute any hand labor was required. I did a horrible thing and yelled at her loud enough that the neighboring troop leader bawled me out. So, I said, "You want her? You take her!" So, this poor woman invited Brittany to be with her troop for a while. She wanted to show us what a kind, patient, and loving troop leader looked like.

When Brittany's adopted troop played volleyball, Brittany wanted to serve all the time…so they let her. When it was time to cook and eat, Brittany wanted hotdogs, and the troop leader had to drive fifteen minutes into town to buy a package of hotdogs. Brittany didn't like the brand she bought so she refused to eat them, then complained of being hungry for the rest of the evening. By the end of the night, all this troop leader's girls were mad at Brittany and complaining to the leader.

We welcomed Brittany back...with conditions. And keeping to the conditions required a lot of perseverance on the part of our troop and me in particular. By the end of the trip, Brittany was starting to be nice and cooperative. It didn't last, but for a while, we thought we might have more cohesion in the group.

The Quality of Wisdom

They say that making unwise decisions results in bad consequences. Making wise decisions results in good consequences. And Wisdom comes from making unwise decisions and learning from them.

It was too easy to just give these Girl Scouts the answers and tell them what to do or not do. There were times they had to fail because wisdom has a cost. There is an art to failure just as there's an art to success. Most motivational speakers will tell you about the art of success—it's about not failing. But that is unreasonable. Success is being true to yourself and making good after failures. In a Budweiser Beer commercial (Anheuser-Busch company) they opined:

*"Men with the spirit of youth pioneered our America...men with vision and sturdy confidence. They found contentment in the thrill of action, knowing that **success was never final and failure never fatal. It was courage that counted.** Isn't the opportunity in America today greater than it was in the days of our grateful forefathers? Good!"*

So, in my years working closely with Lynn and these girls, I had to develop the wisdom to know when to let them fail so they could know how to rise again—humbler but wiser.

Some additional qualities arose from wisdom: Integrity, honesty, perseverance, and patience--some were easily gained, and some were not.

Note to Self: The more painful the lesson the more secure these qualities were imbedded.

The qualities I needed as a leader changed priority depending on the group I was in. Whatever seemed to be the most challenging quality flew to the top of the list. I find this is true even now.

Skills and Knowledge Acquisition

The basis for whatever leadership skills and knowledge always starts with my awareness and my worldview. Then, based on my observations, I must discover the awareness and worldview of the members of the group and the consensus of the group as an organism. I have had to develop a protocol to improve awareness in the people I lead because I cannot MAKE them aware. I re-read this statement, and it seemed unrealistic.

But often, we think the first thing we have to do as a new leader of a group is make them better. What we really need to do is make ourselves better. It's like jumping into a pool.

1. You don't know how deep it is
2. You don't know how cold it is
3. You don't know what's in the water with you.

Here's the thing though. Once you're in the water, you can adapt to the depth, the temperature, and your co-habitants. You do that by learning new skills, discovering new information, and applying what you've acquired from your many experiences in a new way toward a new purpose.

In case you don't have a notebook, let me consolidate what I know about leadership.

SPOTLIGHT ON THE ART OF LEADERSHIP

These are some of the most important notes I've made

- Leadership is facilitating cooperation in the team. Though it may be goal-oriented, the end product is not the purpose of the team, it's cooperating and working together to gain a synergy that makes the end product more than the sum of its parts.

- If you have a good crew, they can solve ALL the problems and successfully complete ALL the projects assigned to them.

- Ask, Don't tell! Questions make your teammates see that you value their input and their intuition. They may surprise you with their insight, creativity, and resourcefulness!

- Seek to bolster morale. Support and praise go a long way to helping a team develop rapport and think together, make use of their strengths, and improve the quality of their work.

- Knowledge of the people is better than knowledge of the work.

- Be Prepared! Pack for every type of weather.

- Make no assumptions about the skill level and knowledge of your team. When in doubt, ASK them! Make sure everyone knows how to set up their tents before leaving on the trip.

- Always plan for challenges...all the way to Plan M. Make plans on how to handle homesickness with the girls early.

- Encourage your teammates to take notes and learn from situations as well! Carry extra small notebooks for people to journal in.

- Keep communication current and regular. Buy postcards at every destination to send home to families during the trip.

- The more painful the lesson the more secure these qualities are imbedded.

Conclusion

I am a better leader now than I was. But many of these notes are especially helpful to followers. My notebook keeps growing and so will yours! The neat thing is that any one of those notes is going to apply to multiple situations which makes it all the more valuable. If you make sure you know that these *Notes to Self* are flexible and serve to make you more conscious of the situation and the people around you, you will never be disappointed.

Reflection Questions

1. When you are in a new leadership position, how would you make use of the "Ask, Don't Tell" principle to build rapport and set goals?

2. What qualities would you want to emphasize in conflict resolution?

3. How could a repository of lessons learned or *Notes to Self* help you in your leadership journey?

4. How would you be able to help your teammates make use of their knowledge and experience to improve the performance of the team?

5. How big an influence does intuition have on your leadership ability?

6. In what way do you remind yourself of the lessons you've learned in your journey? How helpful are the lessons you've observed in other leaders?

2

My Leadership Journey

By: Pamela Hughes

"When you're good to others, you're best to yourself."

~Ben Franklin

Our experiences shape us, including our leadership experiences. Whether we are at the receiving end of other people's leadership behaviors or are at the giving end of providing leadership influence, we can learn and grow. My leadership journey has been a function of emulating leadership performance that has influenced me and sharing my leadership influence with others. The sum total of my leadership journey is summarized with a phrase I repeat often: Model the behavior you want to see in others. It mirrors the Golden Rule. (*Do unto others as you would have them do unto you.*) I try to model the behaviors that have positively affected me and to, in turn, share my knowledge and skills in my interactions. The examples below are milestones along my leadership journey.

The Journey Begins

As a teenager, I was a follower. I was shy and preferred to exist in the background. Being the child of an active military officer, we moved from base to base always leaving friends behind and having to start over. At Dad's last assignment, I went to middle and high school in a small community where most kids had grown up together. It was years before I shed the 'newbie' feeling and even longer to feel as though I had something to contribute.

As a college freshman, I sought and received an invitation from a social organization on campus. I wanted to reinvent myself in this new environment. Little did I know, then, that my first semester was going to be the first step on my leadership journey. Right away, the President of the chapter, an established leader, targeted me to be the leader of the new member group. Why me? What did she see in me? She pulled me aside and told me I was to run for the office. I was impressionable enough, then, to just go along. Why not? My peers voted for me. What did they see in me? I must have filled my semester-long role successfully because I was subsequently encouraged by more senior chapter members to run for a leadership role in the larger chapter. Weren't there others in the chapter who were better positioned to serve? I was still that shy girl, but now I had a push from behind from young women I admired to participate in the world differently.

As a new freshman, I did not ask myself whether I was "ready" for a leadership role, I simply responded to the encouragement of other women. If I had been asked to run for an office instead of being guided into running, I may have declined. As an impressionable 18-year-old eager for acceptance, I did not think declining was an option. Thank goodness! I trusted others who supported and encouraged me as I continued to serve. I am grateful for the leader, the chapter President, who identified something in me that was different than the other 15 new members. She started me on my leadership journey; a journey that hasn't stopped.

My Takeaway: When leaders encourage you to new opportunities, believe them. You are showing them "something" even if you haven't discovered that something yourself.

Who is Ready?

It is relatively easy to influence direct reports or those asking for input. Influencing peers at work may not be as straight forward. Receptiveness to input is an important factor. I love sharing with others about the talents I see in them that they may not be aware of themselves. I also delight in encouraging others to take on new challenges.

As a manager, a frequent scenario was a direct report that I could see was ready for a new challenge, but they did not yet realize their possibilities. New challenges could take the form of learning a new skill, coaching a co-worker, or leading a small project. When discussing the opportunity, I would share why I thought they were ready. I would help them make the connection to their current assignments to what I was proposing. That connection is not always apparent to people focused on performing well in their current role. Encouragement and letting them know what support would be available always proved successful.

For example, a team reorganization created an opening for an application (system) lead on a team that wasn't collaborating well together. I felt that a long-time, accountable team member who had always been in a secondary role was the person for the role. He had the technical background to support the multiple software languages for that application, but he also had the ideal demeanor. I sensed that the team would rally around his good natured, inclusive approach that I had observed in all his work. He and I discussed how I would support him as he established his new role with the challenging team.

A less frequent scenario was when a team member approached me to tell me they were posting for a position in another area to advance their career. Oftentimes, the team member was reluctant to tell me. One humble, competent team member cautiously came to me with this information. Imagine his surprise when I asked about the other position he was considering and what he was looking for with a change to a new position. I was listening for reasons beyond a salary increase. I wanted to understand what growth he envisioned.

We talked through the opportunity, and I encouraged him to interview so that he could learn more about the other team and the new position. He withdrew his name from consideration with the first attempt at a new position. But, about six months later, he came to me to seek advice about another job that looked intriguing. This time, he wasn't reluctant to approach me, but eager to get my perspective.

He got the second job. Bottom line, if the new position were within our company and would further his professional growth, how could I be anything but supportive?

It was sad to see valued team members transition out yet gratifying that I could help with their careers. Several years later, as I was approaching retirement, and this same employee was a fellow Toastmasters club member, he gave a speech about one of his mentors, without naming the mentor. As I listened to him reveal interactions with the mentor, I began to realize that I was that mentor! His generous comments about my impact on him bring tears to my eyes even to this day.

My Takeaway: Encouraging others to use their unique talents or their skills pays off tremendously. *It IS in giving that we receive.* I hope my encouragement inspires those I have encouraged to do the same.

Preparation is Important

One of my first jobs after graduation was in banking. I moved from a "big fish in a little pond" to a "little fish in a big pond." It was personally challenging. I had gotten used to my college peers asking for my input and seeking direction from me. Now, I was a cog in the wheel, not someone that others sought opinion from or considered a leader. Ouch! I had to prove myself. I wasn't mature enough to come to that realization right away. Gradually, after supporting the officers in my department and feeling their confidence in me grow, we developed mutual trust in each other.

A big turning point was when a departing officer shared that he "couldn't have been successful without my help." I was touched by both his sentiment and encouragement. Had I made a difference in someone else's career? He suggested I apply for an open position at his new employer. However, I was also hesitant about his suggestion. Was I ready for that new opportunity? He must have thought so. I trusted him and applied for the new job.

During the interview, it was painfully clear that I could not connect the work I was performing to the federal regulations that determined the processes, and I was not offered the job. In retrospect, I realized that I should have asked why he believed I was qualified. Perhaps the answer would have led me to better prepare for the interview. I was probably flattered by his complimentary comment and was overconfident. However, it has been 30 years since his compliment, and I can still remember exactly how I felt with the conversation. His comments sustained me in later times when I met people who weren't as appreciative of my work.

My Takeaways: When leaders encourage you to new opportunities, ask "Why?" Understanding their perspectives may help in navigating a new path. Heartfelt appreciation makes a difference!

After banking, I moved to a training and project role with a Fortune 500 company and served in team-level lead roles. I was receiving opportunities to exercise my leadership across project teams. But my satisfactory performance was mixed with missteps. My leadership roles were not leading to promotion opportunities, just more of the same. I felt I was ready for the next level of leadership influence, but no one else saw it. Why? Perhaps I wasn't asking the right questions. Perhaps I should have asked: "What is holding me back?" "Why aren't I getting the opportunities that I want?"

Thankfully, one of my managers didn't wait for me to ask and challenged me to improve my communication skills. I had honed my facilitation and presentation skills, but my interpersonal exchanges were too direct. My written communication needed to be reviewed for tone and readability. I was showing "command and control leader" behaviors in a "servant leader" environment. Command and control leadership is characterized by the leader commanding a direction and expecting the team to follow.

While this style was more prevalent years ago, now, it is most common in organizations, such as the military, that are highly structured, hierarchical, and formal. Servant leadership is characterized by the leader facilitating the team to determine their own solutions. It focuses on the growth of the team while concurrently delivering the work.

My manager and I spent 15 minutes over lunch every day discussing my approach to team issues and reviewing my emails. Initially, I was embarrassed. I hoped that my peers didn't notice the extra attention. My embarrassment turned to gratitude after several days when I realized that her attention was helping me. With her coaching, I came to understand why team members and peers were not responding to me as I expected. I began to look forward to our 15 minutes! We only needed to meet for about two weeks before I could "fly" on my own. I was able to understand why my communication skills were holding me back from more significant opportunities. I was so thankful that I got over my initial embarrassment and reluctance and accepted what I could learn from her. This experience helped me to be receptive to input. In fact, another one of my managers later commented "You accept feedback well." I took that as a compliment.

My Takeaway: When your boss wants to invest their own time to help you, be thankful and receptive. Lean into it. If they think their investment in you is worthwhile, so should you.

What helps?
The specificity of my manager's input was very helpful. Instead of offering general advice and examples, we looked at my actual work. Receiving specific input about how to incorporate a softer approach along with the reasoning behind her suggestions helped me to alter my thinking. My altered thinking led to changed behaviors. I have learned to follow this approach when offering feedback.

SPOTLIGHT ON THE ART OF LEADERSHIP

As a long-time Toastmaster, an international communication and leadership building organization, I have had the opportunity to deliver many speech and meeting evaluations over the years. My evaluations are designed to offer two or three pieces of feedback that are both specific and encouraging. Comments pointing out positive points include the "why." For example, instead of saying "Your speech delivery had proper pacing," I might say "Your pacing was ideal. When you needed the audience's attention, you paused before your statement and spoke slowly. I was able to discern your message and keep up before you went to your next point." Providing an exact example with my input not only allows the speaker to know that I appreciated the effect of their cause (proper pacing) but also allows the rest of the club to make that connection too.

Providing input with specificity is even more important when providing developmental feedback regardless of whether the feedback is offered at work or in a Toastmasters club. Developmental feedback is, quite simply, intended to develop the individual. My feedback should reflect that I appreciate the receiver's current skill and care about their personal development. It is a gift that can keep on giving IF it includes the "why." For example, instead of saying, "You looked at your PowerPoint slides on the screen too much," I might say "When you read your slides from the screen, you missed opportunities to connect with your audience." Offering specific feedback that includes the impact is likely to help the receiver better understand your comment.

Delivering feedback to others about Toastmasters projects month after month allowed me to practice giving meaningful feedback to my direct reports in one-on-ones and evaluations. Providing positive feedback is easy. Delivering developmental feedback is not. Not preparing properly produces some of the most uncomfortable discussions ever! I found that giving developmental feedback was easier by including specific details, so the receiver does not have to guess or infer details. I also prepare my input through a caring lens. When I remind myself that I care about the other person's well-being, my preparation is easier, and my delivery is more confident. At times, I practiced delivering difficult feedback for a direct report with a fellow manager. The other manager can give me input as well.

We all have blinders when it comes to our actions. Sometimes our blind spots are small and easily correctable. Other times our blinders shield us from the impact of our actions, and we need others to offer their perspective. Isn't it easier to listen and choose to change behavior when we know that the person offering the feedback genuinely cares about us?

My Takeaway: Be specific with details so that the cause and effect of behaviors or actions is clear. Feedback is a gift to be shared.

Listing is Important Too

It wasn't too long after my manager's individualized coaching sessions before a significant opportunity emerged. I was assigned to a large transformative software program as a project lead over two sub-teams. Leadership on the project expressed confidence in me, but I was filled with self-doubt. I had some past experiences in the business concepts to be transformed, but there was so much that I did not know. During meetings, it seemed everyone else knew what was going on except for me. Why were those in leadership roles expressing confidence in me that I didn't have in myself?

Over time, I started to ask questions and seek clarification. Instead of trying to share what I knew (perhaps to justify my assignment?), I listened more actively and asked better, relevant questions. I paraphrased my understanding to ensure accuracy. As my knowledge grew, I began to have more confidence in my team. They were the experts; I was the process facilitator. I needed to trust their information to assess progress and emerging issues. As my own understanding grew, their openness grew too. Our communication became bi-directional; each of us was responsible for listening and asking questions. We needed to actively engage in discussions to tackle issues and understand progress. As our team communication dynamics grew, our trust in each other and our individual roles grew as well. Our trust became bi-directional too.

> My Takeaway: Listen to understand, not to be heard. Trust across the team does wonders for team effectiveness. Team members will engage when they realize you are listening, and they are trusted.

Unfortunately, our program met issues that led to a re-examination of the initial assumptions and cost projections. I participated in many analysis and replanning sessions. I had learned to listen to and ask thoughtful, relevant questions during break-out sessions. I had also learned not to speak up if I did not have productive input.

I saw most of my fellow project managers resisting the needed changes. They objected to the re-vamped program both overtly and subtly. Overtly resisting by not being open to issue identification and problem-solving. Subtly resisting by asking leading questions designed to highlight their pet peeves. I even saw grimacing and sneering. The decision makers, of course, noticed and the objectors' assignments soon ended.

With the role changes, I realized that leaders need team members with "can do" attitudes. A "cannot" attitude isn't acceptable, especially when changes are required. I was retained in a program support role, but most project lead roles were outsourced to a consulting firm. I wanted a more influential role than my immediate assignment and hoped that it would evolve into a more challenging role. To display my "can do" attitude, I was conscious about how I responded to all the issues that crop up in large software projects.

> My Takeaway: When changes are warranted, be receptive. There is always a place at the table for people who want to contribute productively.

Perspectives
My receptiveness to my new role and my improved communication skills led to opportunities to spend more time in meetings with program leaders, especially the two Senior Vice Presidents sponsoring the program. Over the course of the next two years, I was afforded one-on-one time with both women, and I welcomed their mentoring.

Early on, in program meetings, I heard them ask questions that weren't directly related to the information offered. I could not understand why they asked what appeared, to me, to be unrelated questions. I was confused about why their questions were not about the underlying work processes. Why wasn't senior leadership interested in the details? Hearing a question that I didn't understand, I began to think "What was the intent behind the question?" "How was the information important to a senior leader?" I also carefully asked these types of questions in one-on-ones with my mentors.

I started to realize that information that was relevant to a Senior Vice President was not the same information that was relevant to a mid-level project manager. They were interested in the wheat, not the chaff. They were interested in the results, not the finer details along the route. Could I learn to eliminate the chaff from my statements? Could I report "Z" without slogging my audience from "A to Z?" Executives do not have time for the details. They want the results. I began to understand the value of reporting about the result (the What) and not about the process (the How). I began to practice those concepts myself and take coaching from them in my written reports.

My contributions to the program grew and soon my role was recognized as the Program Manager, not just program support. While that recognition did not come with a formal job title change, just a role description, it did represent more visibility across the program. No longer was I relaying information to an intermediary for executive-level communications. I was that intermediary.

I was facilitating activities with project leaders, my former peers in the program. I was listening to my peers' report about results, progress, and issues. I was paying attention to the unsaid cues that could expose gaps. Gaps that could, hopefully, be addressed earlier rather than later. With my understanding of the kind of details that were important to executives, I was learning to view issues through the project sponsor's lens, representing their needs instead of my own. Eventually, I was communicating to the Chief Information Officer about progress.

My Takeaways: Customize your message to your audience. Executives operate on a higher plane of information needs than the "doers." Value one-on-one time with senior leaders. They want to help and will invest their time when they see promise.

When I was promoted to a formal leadership role (a manager), I experienced this same scenario as the leader who now just needed to know the end results, not every action taken or every issue that was encountered to produce results.

Now that I was on the receiving end of what I considered superfluous information, but which my team thought was relevant, I had an important insight: the details were about trust. Team members think leaders want all the fine details because they believe the leader may not trust their work. But, of course, good servant leaders should and do trust their expert team members.

It was up to me, as the leader manager, to ask about the results, not tasks. I also needed to carefully steer the discussion away from the nonvalue-added details. It is not easy to re-direct team members who are passionate about the details of their work. Assuring them that they had my trust was an on-going process.

> My Takeaway: Communication can be more streamlined when we recognize the trust we have for each other. Trust can take time, but building it is worthwhile.

Appreciate Yourself
The growth I experienced while assigned to that large software program was an inflection point both personally and professionally. I felt valued. I was no longer a cog-in-the-wheel, but an influencer. My visibility across the company had grown as my leadership responsibilities had widened. The confidence I had in myself began to match the confidence that others had in me. I started to believe I was ready for a new role in formal leadership. I connected how what I had learned in a project leadership role could translate into a positional leadership role.

As the Program was winding down, my mentors both encouraged me to consider posting for a manager position on one of the new teams being formed. Much earlier in my career, I had failed to prepare myself fully when encouraged to apply for a new position. I had failed to ask, "why do you think I'm ready?" I was not going to make the same mistake. Their answers helped me to realize the value of all the lessons I had learned and what qualities were important to them as senior positional leaders. Plus, it helped that they were half of the interview team! Applying their input to the interview questions allowed me to feel confident in the skills and experiences that I could bring to the position. Behavioral interview questions that begin with "Tell me about a time that you..." require preparation. Their input and my homework paid off and I got the job.

My Takeaways: Retrospectively take time to evaluate what you have learned and the experiences you have gained. Realizing the impact of our growth may not be easily apparent. Growth is not only additive, but cumulative. Hopefully, what is learned becomes the new standard.

What Else Could I Share?

Many of my leadership lessons and experiences have been learned on the job, but I have also gathered skills and learned lessons while serving in Toastmasters leadership roles. Because there is less positional authority, volunteer leadership must rely on collaboration, persuasion, and interpersonal relationships. Yes, these are the same characteristics that are valuable in paid positions but are paramount in volunteer roles. Some lessons are the same; some are different.

For example, in club leadership, I transitioned from serving as an officer to mentoring other officers in a company-based club. There were many times when I called a member to encourage them to serve as an officer and shared with them how this volunteer activity could translate to their job duties or desired position. Their initial reluctance about committing to additional responsibilities turned into receptiveness when I helped them understand the benefits. I enjoyed identifying an emerging leader, providing encouragement, and then watching them perform the role that I had suggested. Because of the more limited scope of a club officer's role compared to their paid position, I observed their growth over a shorter duration than what was achievable at the same time within their paid position.

I was at the receiving end of that a similar type of encouragement while serving in a financial role at the broader, district level. The director said we would be on the leading edge of piloting new financial processes in the global organization. He had confidence in my abilities to implement and pointed out the benefits to the district and to me personally. I suppose I had the option to say, 'no thank you', but I had already learned to lean in to new challenges. I was proud to know that we were one of the first districts in the world to make the change and had done so smoothly. I was happy to help shape the direction of the larger rollout to other districts.

One concept that is different in volunteer organizations is motivation. Whether you volunteer for a task or take on a larger role, our motivations for doing so are intrinsic. We are not taking on added responsibilities because there's a financial payoff, we do so for more qualitative benefits. Maybe the volunteer wants to meet new people, advance skills they cannot exercise in a paid role, or simply to challenge themselves with something new and different. As a leader in a volunteer organization, I have learned to manage my own expectations about results. For example, if there are gaps in what volunteers know, partnering them with another volunteer is usually successful and more enjoyable

My Takeaways: Offering encouragement is no different in for-profit companies than it is in volunteer organizations. Meet people "where they're at." A volunteer may not have the ideal skills needed or understand the time commitments involved in an activity or new role. But they can and will contribute. Don't discount what the individual can offer.

Not always the Leader

As someone who is often called upon to fulfill a team lead role in both paid and volunteer positions, I also relish it when I am not the leader. When I can be the valued team member who says what they're going to do and then does it. The valued team member who can offer ideas and will support a better idea from the group. The valued team player who can help, behind the scenes, others on the team. After all, as someone who has led many initiatives, I know what a good team player looks and acts like. And I know what the leader expects from a contributing team player. I have enjoyed supporting peers as they exercise their leadership capabilities and have tried to make their job easier

My Takeaway: The best way to be a good leader is to also be a good team player.

Mixed Success

One may conclude that I have been able to successfully incorporate most leadership characteristics into how I approach the roles I have held. Unfortunately, learning to be an effective leader is not an easy stroll, but a winding uphill trek. There are setbacks, a couple of which I have shared here. There are also leadership characteristics that I have not successfully incorporated into my skillset.

I have not mastered delegation. Most people struggle to delegate, so I am not alone. Often, the leader may believe they can do the work just as well or better than the team member, so the leader completes the task themselves. I identify with this thinking, but my reasoning goes even deeper. I have served in many administrative roles and have gathered a lot of knowledge, skills, and abilities along the way. When I see tasks that will allow me to incrementally stretch my skill set, I tend to keep those activities for myself, even though they may not be leader-level activities. I want to learn something new too! I realize my selfishness in wanting that sense of accomplishment for myself. I could be preventing someone else from having that experience or learning something new. I have resigned myself to the knowledge that delegation is not my strong suit.

Managing my command-and-control leadership tendency is another challenging area. Awareness has been helpful and, when I have come on too strong, a warm, genuine, caring smile always saves the day. I try to delegate more and show less control but have chosen to spend my energy developing deeper acuity in the leadership areas that interest me

My Takeaway: Know yourself. Appreciate what you do well. Don't beat yourself up for shortcomings. Accept them and excel at what comes more naturally.

The Journey Continues

Throughout my professional and volunteer careers, there have been pivotal experiences that shaped who I became as a leader. As I observed and learned from formal and informal leaders over the years, I have tried to exhibit the same leadership traits with others that made such a meaningful impression on me. Asking "why?" served me well as I navigated new scenarios, roles, and challenges. I hope that I have been an example of my mantra: Model the behavior that you want to see in others. After all, my expectations of others should be the same as my expectations of myself, right?

I have enjoyed developing strategies and plans, leading teams as we execute plans, and motivating and influencing. I have enjoyed being "large and in charge" and accountable even as I learned to be a servant leader for my teams. As I came to the end of my professional career and multi-year volunteer leadership role, I have realized that the leadership roles I enjoy the most are those working in one-on-one situations. For example, matching assignments with an individual's background or matching an assignment with an individual's desired growth are so satisfying.

Helping struggling team members who can't see a way forward on an issue or lending my input was always the best part of my day. I have enjoyed helping associates realize how the team or volunteer leadership roles they have fulfilled apply to the positions they aspire to. It has been gratifying to help them understand how to communicate their growth to managers and then watch them move into promotions. My leadership journey continues and will revolve around helping others in fulfilling their goals. Just as leaders along my journey have influenced how I exercise my leadership skills, I hope I have and will continue to influence others as they develop.

Reflection Questions

1. Do you have an example of when someone else had confidence in your leadership capabilities that you did not have? Did you take their encouragement and act on it?

2. Have you taken a leadership role that didn't end well? What happened?

3. What was the most valuable coaching you received?

4. What was the best mentor relationship you've had? What made it good?

3

Leadership, Naturally

By Randy Prier

"Some are born leaders, some achieve leadership, and some have leadership thrust upon them."
~Maurice Flanagan,

"There go the people. I must follow them, for I am their leader."
~ Alexandre Auguste Ledru-Rollin

Introduction
"Some are born leaders, . . ."

Growing up, I was a good student, fairly articulate when I spoke, and an avid reader. (Can you say "nerd?") Doing well seemed to come naturally. So, teachers and other adult mentors tended to steer me toward special opportunities. In fact, I have been involved in leadership roles for most of my life. Some I pursued, but many pursued me.

.

SPOTLIGHT ON THE ART OF LEADERSHIP

Junior High and High School

Early on I developed an interest in American history and politics, focusing on my hero Abraham Lincoln and other great presidents. When the 1960 presidential election came between the sitting Vice President, Richard Nixon, and John F. Kennedy, the attractive, inspiring young senator from Massachusetts I was enthralled. I reveled in the horse race, the advertising and the first-ever televised presidential debates. A local department store was selling large, picture campaign buttons for both tickets. I eagerly bought some and displayed them in my room at home.

Soon after the annual City Government Day in the city's junior high schools occurred. This program was designed to help young people learn about the city government and how it worked. When I found out that students could run in mock elections for Mayor, City Council, and other municipal positions, this was my chance to engage in a campaign something like the 1960 presidential election, though obviously on a much smaller scale. I was hooked and decided to run for Mayor from my school. I threw myself into the race, giving speeches and producing my own handmade posters and buttons (on card stock) with corny slogans like, "If you're in a rut or stuck in the mire, help yourself and vote for Prier!" I was running against the most popular girl in class, who I think mostly relied on that popularity. I won handily. This wasn't a real leadership position, since the winners just went to spend a day in City Hall learning about the city government and how it functioned. But I was thrilled to participate.

Lesson learned: First, if there's something you really want, put your whole self into the process. Win or lose, you'll learn a lot and benefit from the experience. Second, many times the journey to something is much more satisfying than the end goal. Finally, after later losing an election for Student Council president to a popular fellow student, I learned that popularity will win if you don't reach out and make connections with the people making the decision.

College.

". . . some achieve leadership. . ."

As a freshman I joined a group of off-campus independents called the University of Nebraska Independent Cornhuskers, or UNICORNS. We considered ourselves to be the independents' answer to fraternities and sororities. We met weekly, held regular parties, conducted service projects and invited speakers on a variety of interesting topics to our meetings. These things were a welcome break from classes and schoolwork and a chance to socialize, so I got into the activities of the club in a big way, particularly the parties and the special speakers.

In the middle of my junior year, I was elected President of the club, the term carrying over into the fall semester next year. Things went well; however, I felt that holding elections in the middle of the school year put the new officers at a disadvantage as they tried to get up to speed in the midst of the spring semester. So, I proposed that we move the elections to the end of the school year in June. This, I thought would allow the new officers to settle into their positions over the summer and hit the ground running in the fall. To facilitate the transition, I proposed that the current officers, including me, continue in office until the end of the school year. Much to my surprise, a lot of the members vigorously protested the proposal. They seemed to think I was on an ego trip, that my proposal was a power grab (as if a few more months in office was such a big deal). I'll admit I enjoyed being president of the club, but I didn't see this coming. I felt I had done a good job and was just trying to make things easier for the folks coming after me.

> **Lesson learned:** Once again, perhaps my "loner" nature kept me from accurately reading the crowd. I still hadn't learned that networking to gain support from group members is a necessary leadership skill.

One other thing happened in college that changed my life and leadership experience. A requirement for graduation at the University was you either had to take a couple of semesters of physical education or a year in one of the military Reserve Officer Training Corps (ROTC) programs. I wasn't too athletic, so my high school friends and I decided to enroll in the Air Force ROTC (the Air Force seemed more palatable than either the Army or the Navy).

There was no intention of making a career in the Air Force. I was going to become a lawyer and use that as an entry into electoral politics. However, once in the program, I learned that if you agreed to continue in ROTC for four years, earning a commission as a Second Lieutenant (2d Lt) and had a good academic record you could earn a scholarship covering your last two years as an undergrad (I had a Regents scholarship for the first two years but could sure use help in financing the rest of my education.) Beyond that, this was in the mid-60's during the height of the Vietnam War. Every young male my age had to deal with the possibility of being drafted. Because of my myopic eyes I wasn't going to be a pilot, and being some kind of Air Force support officer seemed a lot more attractive than being an Army "ground pounder." (My apologies to any Army people.)

I decided to go for the ROTC scholarship, earn my BA degree and be commissioned. Then I'd get a delay from entering active duty, go to law school and become a lawyer in the Air Force for the required four years on active duty. That was the plan, and it worked--until I got into law school and found out I really didn't like the law. It was only ever meant as a path into politics. I hadn't even considered what kind of law I would practice. So, I quit law school and went on into the Air Force. Career plans after that were now up in the air.

Air Force.

". . . and some have leadership thrust upon them."

My first duty station was at Keesler Air Force Base (AFB) in Biloxi, Mississippi. Keesler is a training base primarily for first-term airmen. My assigned career field was as an Administration Management/ Executive Support Officer. This is a broad career field covering a wide assortment of jobs from information management (read paperwork) to direct support of senior military and civilian officers.

After a two-month training course in entry-level duties for my career field I was given my first job with actual responsibilities in the real world. It was as the administrative officer for one of the several student airmen squadrons on the base. The admin officer is the second-ranking person in a squadron, effectively the deputy commander.

I really don't remember being nervous as I stepped into this role. For one thing, having had two years in law school, there had been about three years since my commissioning. So, I was given credit for time in grade as a 2nd Lt and therefore promoted to 1st Lt after only a month on active duty. This gave me a tad more respect from others than a "butter-bar" normally gets. ("Butter-bar" is a slightly dismissive term referring to the gold color of a 2nd Lt's rank insignia.) More importantly, my commander was another 1st Lt, who had been around for a while and could show me the ropes.

However, the primary work of supervising the daily activities of the student airmen and maintaining discipline outside of the classroom was done by a staff of experienced Non-Commissioned officers (NCOs/sergeants) in a Training Office. In addition, the senior NCO assigned, usually a Master Sergeant, is called the First Sgt. He is a primary advisor to the squadron commander, a coordinator between the commander and the Training Office sergeants, and a sort of "father figure" for all the enlisted personnel in the squadron.

The military services have a somewhat unique personnel structure. In most large organizations, middle managers and staff officers are people who have worked their way up through the ranks. In the military, however, the most experienced people in middle management are the senior NCOs, particularly in non-combat support functions. But their nominal supervisors are lightly experienced company-grade officers (lieutenants and captains). Consequently, young officers who are officially superior in rank are effectively trained on-the-job by NCOs.

While at Keesler, I served in three different student squadrons and became commander of the third one. During that time, I learned a lot about how the Air Force worked and grew to respect the knowledge and experience of the NCOs in the squadrons. For example, in a previous ABC book, "Spotlight on the Art of Confidence," I described how the NCOs in that last squadron came to me with a proposal to rearrange the airmen in the barracks by their training shift so that the comings and goings of the different shifts would not disturb each other. The proposal made complete sense and so I was happy to approve it.

> **Lesson learned**: Smart young lieutenants certainly have to have good judgement and assess the capabilities and dependability of the NCOs who work for them, but they also must listen to and trust their NCOs' experience.

In the second of the student squadrons I served in, my commander—Capt. K, I'll call him--was a pilot who had been giving flight training to young South Vietnamese pilot candidates there at Keesler. I believe he was given the student squadron assignment as a means of broadening his experience in anticipation of possible future command assignments. Capt. K was a "gung-ho" type who took the attitude that as commander, his word was law. When situations came up that didn't suit him, he tended to get angry, loud and demanding. One day, he called a young airman into his office which I shared. This young man had been hiding in the barracks and skipping class. As Capt. K interrogated the airman, who I believe had come from an underprivileged background, the airman grew defiant, stood up and ran out of the office. Capt. K shouted at the airman to come back, but he didn't. The Capt.'s immediate response was to start discharge procedures—no attempt to counsel or rehabilitate the airman. So, the airman lost a chance to improve his lot in life, and the Air Force lost a potentially valuable member.

On later reflection, I believe the captain manifested this behavior as the result of a lack of empathy for others and perhaps as a way to cover some lack of confidence in what he was doing.

> **Lesson learned**: An effective leader should show some understanding of his people's feelings and at least try to modify their behavior.

I've spent a lot of time on my first Air Force assignments because they were foundational to my real-world experiences in the military. But in several of my next assignments I wasn't actually in a position of leadership. I did have the opportunity to observe the leaders I served under.

My first overseas assignment was to Clark Air Base in the Philippines. While there I had two different jobs, first as an Assistant Protocol Officer for the 13th Air Force Headquarters and the 405th Fighter Wing, then as Assistant Director of Administration for 13th Air Force. All of my bosses there were very competent and great to work for, but I especially remember the Commander of the 405th Fighter Wing, Colonel G. He had a high-pressure job but was very personable and likeable. At the time I wore a mustache which I kept well within Air Force appearance standards. I sensed the colonel didn't like it, but by regulation he couldn't tell me to shave it off. He could have applied some unofficial pressure on me but didn't. I really liked Colonel Gordon, so I decided to shave off the mustache. The colonel's reaction was to laugh and say, "Oh, Randy, that looks so much better!" After that I respected him all the more.

> **Lesson learned:** Even while setting and enforcing standards, leaders can gain more regard and better results by being cordial and respectful of their subordinates.

A subsequent assignment was to the Defense Intelligence Agency (DIA) in Washington, DC. The job was an administrative position in DIA's Directorate of Estimates (DE). DE's analysts studied intelligence reports from around the world and prepared estimates of foreign countries' military capabilities, weapon systems and strategies. The admin section's work involved controlling a lot of highly classified documents as well as handling budgetary and personnel matters for the directorate. My boss was a senior military civilian officer, Mr. H., who was personable and easy to get along with, but who tended to be something of a micromanager. Every morning those of us in the administrative section would meet in Mr. H.'s office where he would hand out new assignments and then go over our progress on previously assigned tasks in detail. I think I performed well but the way Mr. H hovered over us led me to believe that I wasn't fully trusted. Consequently, all of us in the admin section were hesitant to show initiative or suggest different ways of doing things.

I think part of Mr. H's mode of operation was due to his ambition to be promoted before he retired. He didn't want any mistakes made that could damage his chances. Therefore, he passed on the pressure he felt to us. When the promotion didn't happen, Mr. H retired. The civilian officers who replaced him tended to trust us in the admin office a little more.

Lesson learned: A leader who clearly sets expectations and trusts his subordinates to meet them—only correcting when necessary—will likely achieve better results than one who gets directly involved in every detail.

SPOTLIGHT ON THE ART OF LEADERSHIP

"There go the people. I must follow them, for I am their leader."

My next assignment was to the Headquarters of the Air Force Office of Special Investigations (AFOSI) located on Bolling Air Force Base, in Washington, DC.

AFOSI is the Air Force's version of the FBI. The headquarters supervises AFOSI detachments on every Air Force Base around the world. Their job is to investigate the more serious crimes than those handled by the Security Police on a base and those cases involving senior officers.

My job was to be the Director of Administration (DA) for the headquarters. DA operated programs such as communications, records, regulations publishing, and reproduction management. It also ran a word processing center where all the headquarters correspondence, reports, and regulations were typed. (This was in the early stages of electronic information processing and just before the introduction of personal computers, electronic networks and the Internet.)

This was the first time that I was actually in charge of a good-sized organization with around 30 people, both military and civilian. The thing is that all of my Division Chiefs were either senior NCOs or civilians who had a lot of experience. And, as the headquarters of a special Air Force office, when replacements were required, AFOSI usually had its pick of pretty well-qualified people. This isn't to say that we had no problems, but for the most part AFOSI/DA was a well-oiled machine. Consequently, managing the directorate was not a tremendously difficult job. It pretty much ran itself.

I always felt like DA wasn't given much respect by the rest of the AFOSI headquarters. I think we were taken for granted as mere factotums by the career agents who filled the most important HQ positions. For one thing, the position I held was rated to be filled by a Lieutenant Colonel (Lt Col), but as noted earlier I was a major as was my predecessor. This was a tacit sign that we were considered to be second-class citizens, particularly since there didn't seem to be any interest on the part of the organization's leadership to push for getting a Lt Col assigned, though that may have given us a bit more respect within the HQ. We did our jobs, but it was like we weren't actually part of the group.

Lesson learned: When you aren't totally accepted as a true part of the organization you're in, buckle down and do your job as well as you can. Hopefully, things will improve.

Subsequently, I was fortunate to be selected for a special assignment called Education With Industry (EWI). As the name implies this program places qualified officers with major US companies to learn about their technologies and methods of management related to the career field of the assignee. My assignment was with the administration division of the 3M Company in St Paul, Minnesota. This division was in the beginning steps of developing what would later evolve into the Internet-based administrative and technical networks that all companies employ today. This was in the early 80's, so the Internet was still in its infancy. Thus, the division was busy evaluating evolving word processing and personal computer systems that could be used to streamline information management throughout the company. I was exposed to some of the state-of-the-art computer systems coming into use, as well the development of the techniques for designing and managing these systems. This was a fascinating several months.

Once an EWI participant from the AF/DA community completes the tour with their assigned company, they would be placed in the administration complement in the headquarters of one of the Air Force major commands/organizations. Consequently, I was assigned to the Headquarters, Strategic Air Command (SAC) Directorate of Administration (DA), at Offutt AFB, close to Omaha, Nebraska. My position was Chief of SAC/DA's Plans and Programs Division. This small office of only five people handled DA's participation in all kinds of special HQ programs such as organizational and policy planning, personnel staffing, budgeting, and, more specifically, deployment of administrative personnel during Operation Desert Shield/Storm against Iraq.

All of my people were very experienced and qualified, so there really wasn't a lot of supervision involved other than assigning projects, reviewing work products, and rating personnel performance. Overall, I think our small group did an outstanding job. We must have been doing something good since I was promoted to Lieutenant Colonel.

Perhaps the most interesting assignment of my Air Force career was as the Liaison Officer between the Air Force's Third Air Division (3AD) on Andersen Air Base, and the Government of the Island of Guam, an American Territory in the Western Pacific. In this multifaceted position I maintained contact between my boss, the Commander of 3AD (a Major General) and the Governor's office, the Territorial Legislature, the island's village governments, Guam's Congressional Delegate, and the Philippine and Japanese consuls. I also held an ex-officio position on the Island's Board of Education because the island's school system provided elementary and secondary schooling for the children of US military personnel assigned to Guam.

The island's public schools were frankly not very good because of inadequate funding, poorly trained teachers, and subpar maintenance of school buildings in Guam's subtropical climate. To be honest, the laid-back nature of the island culture didn't seem to give a very high priority to public education, and these conditions obviously didn't sit very well with military parents. While the Department of Defense (DoD) runs a high-quality system of elementary/high schools on our overseas bases, bases on US territories rely on the schools run by the territories. This put me in a tough spot, trying to defend Guam's schools to parents while at the same time making the case for improvements for our kids (including my own son and daughter) before the school board.

After receiving complaints from military parents, DoD Schools initiated a contract with Guam authorities under which DoD would provide funding for educational upgrades in return for program improvements by Guam authorities. The contract went through; however, it was going to take time for any progress to begin showing. In the meantime, meetings with parents to explain the contract effort remained contentious. I'm afraid I didn't do a very good job of assuaging the parents' feelings. I was perhaps a little too defensive of the DoD effort. The parents wanted DoD schools right then!

Lesson learned: In a tense situation where feelings are running high, a leader needs to show empathy for the points of view of everyone involved. He should try to stick to the facts and be as impartial as possible.

Upon completion of the Guam assignment, I returned to HQ Strategic Command in the same position I held before. This was my final Air Force assignment since I stayed there until retirement in early 1993.

Toastmasters.
In early 1981, while I was assigned to HQ AFOSI, I joined Toastmasters International, a worldwide membership organization dedicated to helping its members develop and improve their communication and leadership skills. A fellow officer on the AFOSI staff, Major Joe Corwin, was president of the Toastmasters club on Bolling Air Force Base, and he encouraged me to visit one of the club's meetings.

Most people join Toastmasters to help them become more confident and skilled at speaking in public. I had been a high school and college debater, so I didn't think I needed any help in that area. However, once I visited the club, I realized how much I liked having the opportunity to speak, delivering interesting and informative messages. I especially enjoyed making people laugh. At the same time, I learned that for the club to succeed and members to achieve their personal growth goals everyone had to take an active part in the meetings and in the management of the club. In the meetings, for example there was a Toastmaster who ran that day's program, and each assigned speaker had an evaluator who gave the speaker feedback on how they performed. Officers elected by the members ran the club.

The Spring after I joined, Joe Corwin entered one of the annual Toastmasters speech contest cycles, winning at the succeeding club, area, and division levels. That qualified him to participate in the district-level contest, and I signed up to go to the District Conference where he would be speaking. Unfortunately, Joe didn't win, but I was enthralled with the event. I made a commitment to myself to participate in the contests as soon as I could which would eventually become a goal to win the Toastmasters International Speech Contest at a District level (a goal I finally achieved several years later).

In addition to the speech contest, I was also very impressed by the personal presence and air of command of the District Governor, the elected leader of the district which included the area around Washington, DC. He was a large man with a leonine mane of dark red hair. He was so smooth and completely in charge of all the proceedings of that district conference. I told myself, "Gee, I'd like to be like him," and over time I developed a goal to become a district governor (another goal that I later achieved).

After that initial exposure to Toastmasters, I've always been a member of at least one Toastmasters club wherever I was, and I've almost always been a club officer. Before leaving for Guam, I completed a term as an Area Governor, the leader of the next organizational level above the club. While in Guam I earned my first Distinguished Toastmaster (DTM) Award, the organization's highest educational designation. I've since earned two more DTMs. After returning from Guam, the District 24 Governor who was also an officer on the HQ SAC staff asked me to become the Lieutenant Governor (Lt Gov) for one of District 24's Divisions. That started my climb up to the top three District chairs, as the following year I was elected District 24's Administrative Lt Gov, followed by Lt Gov for Education, then District Governor in 1992, as noted above.

Lesson learned: Toastmasters is a very goal-oriented organization using programs with specific objectives at every level. These programs are designed so that you only achieve your objectives by helping others achieve theirs. As a leader this helped me learn the importance of well-defined goals as well as the methods and interdependency among organizational members required to achieve them.

SPOTLIGHT ON THE ART OF LEADERSHIP

I enjoyed all of the offices I held in Toastmasters, but probably the most fulfilling was my year as District Governor. That year the leadership of Toastmasters International decided to raise an individual member's dues—they had not been raised for several years. This had the predictable effect of many members deciding not to renew their membership. Since one of the goals for becoming a Distinguished District was membership growth of at least three percent over the preceding year, our prospects of achieving Distinguished District status became very slim.

Two months before the end of the year, I had almost given up hope. But then the Toastmasters Board of Directors saw that the likely effect of the dues increase would be that few districts around the world would make Distinguished. This would be a bad look for the organization, so the Board decided to suspend the membership growth goal for one year. The other goals for the number of educational awards and growth in the number of clubs stayed in effect.

This decision gave us new life, but, while we had achieved the goals for educational awards, it didn't look like we would have enough clubs. So, I went to work and contacted all of the clubs that looked shaky. With a great deal of persuasion and the help of other district leaders, including past district governors, I succeeded in getting enough clubs to add the members required to remain in good standing. It was one of the proudest moments of my life when later that summer I received the news that we had qualified for Distinguished status.

Later that summer, at the Toastmasters International Convention in Toronto, I triumphantly raised the Distinguished District plaque above my head. To this day it still hangs on the wall in our living room. It wasn't so much a personal award, but a recognition of the personal improvements achieved by the members of our district.

For several years after being District Governor I didn't hold any offices outside of the clubs I belonged to, but over time my ambitious nature led me to decide to go for election to the Toastmasters International Board of Directors. This would require me to campaign first for the endorsement of the other districts within our region (the next level of the organization above the district) through phone calls and personal visits to the district conferences. I was favorably received by these district leaders and won their endorsement with a strong majority at the business meeting in the Regional Convention.

The final elections for the Board were held in August 2001, at the International Convention in Anaheim, California. There I spoke to hundreds of people, participated in a candidates showcase (sort of like a mass interview) and gave a brief campaign speech at the business meeting. I was fortunate to receive over 55 percent of the vote against another strong candidate. This was another most gratifying moment of my life.

Work on the Board was intense. We were required to review several continuing programs in the organization and recommend changes. One that I worked on was the rules for speech contests. I recommended some changes that I thought would make the contests fairer. These were adopted. There were two directors from each Region serving overlapping two-year terms, and we were also required to visit all of the districts within our region between us each year. These went well.

One of the biggest challenges I faced during my term on the board was that three of the districts in our Region were falling below the minimum number of clubs required to remain an independent district. They each had been given three years to bring their totals up to the minimum requirement of 60 clubs but had not succeeded. So, the Board decided to merge these three districts into one.

It was up to my partner director and me to convene a meeting of the leadership trios of all three districts to work out the details of the transition. This was a difficult meeting because none of the three districts were happy with the prospect of merging. But by listening carefully to their concerns while holding steadfast to the necessity and broad outlines of the process, we were able to agree on what to do. After that, at the Regional convention in June, just before the transition was to take effect, we had to address what was happening and face the lingering resentment. I put the best face on the project that I could, and most people ultimately resigned themselves to the inevitable.

My two years on the Board went very quickly, but I enjoyed every moment. During those two years we met during the International Conventions held in Anaheim, San Antonio, and Atlanta, all delightful places to visit. We also met in the luxuriously appointed Boardroom in the beautiful world headquarters in Santa Ana, California. Beyond that we enjoyed a close comradeship amongst all the Board members.

Lesson learned: As a Toastmaster leader I learned the importance of collaborative and consensual decision-making, even when there were the inevitable conflicting opinions. This served me well when I served as the director of our church's annual Last Supper Easter play for almost 20 years, and later when I was picked to lead the steering committee for a major capital campaign to raise funds for the construction of a new church building. Both efforts were eminently successful.

Conclusions

I feel like I have had a successful career as a leader, although like most people I suppose, I have regrets. Perhaps the biggest is that, despite my successes, I don't feel I have fully lived up to my potential. I am secure, though, in the knowledge that I have affected the lives of a number of people in a positive way. I haven't gotten along with everyone I have met, but that number is small. As far as lessons learned about leadership, I have commented on most of them throughout this chapter.

By definition, leadership is the ability to influence and guide members of a team in achieving the group's mission or goals. Leaders are seen as people who make sound and sometimes difficult decisions. They articulate a clear vision, establish achievable goals and provide followers with the knowledge and tools necessary to achieve those goals.

However, most of the leadership training I received wasn't truly about how to be a leader. In the Air Force you were automatically deemed to be a leader by virtue of the rank insignia you wore. However, most of what I learned was transactional. This is what you did in this or that situation. This was how you filled out the paperwork and who you had to coordinate with. There was virtually nothing about how to set goals and generate buy-in to those goals, how to motivate your people, counsel them to perform better or resolve conflicts. I found this to be true in most of my "leadership" situations to come. But in general, I think my instincts served me well, and I learned most of what I know by observing others. On the whole I am satisfied.

SPOTLIGHT ON THE ART OF LEADERSHIP

Reflection Questions

1. If you have been a leader of any kind of team, group, or organization, were you given any kind of formal training for that position? If so, did you find the training helpful in pursuing the mission of the organization and dealing with any problems that came up?

2. If you were not formally trained as a leader, how did you learn to lead? Did you find that method effective.?

3. Think back on all the leaders you served under. Who was/were your favorite(s)? What was their approach to leadership and why did you like the way they led?

4. Who were your least favorite leaders? What about them made you feel that way?

5. What were the most useful lessons you have learned from your leadership experiences, both as a leader and a follower? What made them useful?

4

A Tale of Two (Leadership) Journeys

By: Mark Fegan

"Anyone who loves sausage or the law should not watch either being made."

~W. Rogers

"A journey of a thousand miles begins with a single step."

~Tao Te Ching (Book of Tao)

"There is no royal road to Geometry."

~Euclid

"Leaders Lead – Followers Follow"

~anon

Over the course of my life, I have filled a number of leadership positions, some elected and some appointed. In each case, I learned valuable lessons about leadership and the process of leading.

To clarify things, an appointed position is one for which you are asked to serve in a leadership position; your appointment may be confirmed by the organization but that is not a requirement for the appointment. An elected position is one where you are nominated for a leadership position with the organization and are elected to the position by a vote of the members of that organization.

As examples of each type of leadership position, consider two of the early leadership positions I filled:

1. My senior year in high school, I was first chair and section leader for my high school band's cornet section. As section leader, I was responsible for leading a weekly rehearsal of the cornet section. I was appointed to this position by the band director.

2. After graduating from college, I started my professional career as a secondary school Mathematics teacher; I taught in several school districts in Minnesota and Nebraska. At each school, I was a member of the local chapter of the National Education Association (NEA). While at my final

secondary teaching position, with a medium sized school district in extreme southeast Nebraska, I was President of the local NEA chapter. This was an elected position.

A question that comes to mind is "What did I do to prepare for each of these leadership opportunities?" Or, perhaps more importantly, "What can I do to prepare for leadership opportunities I may encounter in the future?"

Leadership by Appointment or Promotion from Within

First a bit of additional background. The high school I attended in west central Minnesota was home to one of the best high school bands in the state. We were primarily a concert band although we did march in several parades each year and provided a pep band for football and basketball games.

A large part of the success of the band was the use of sectional rehearsals to supplement the regular band rehearsals. The band was divided into sections, usually by instrument: cornets, flutes, clarinets, and so on. Each section met weekly, outside of the regular rehearsal time. These sectional rehearsals allowed members a chance to get peer assistance while mastering the music. Sectional rehearsals were led by section leaders, generally the top players in their sections.

As a high school senior, I became the section leader for the cornet section. Bear in mind, I had no formal training on how to be a section leader. I was appointed to the position in part because I was the most experienced player in the section. I was the only cornet player in my junior high school graduating class who continued with instrumental music after entering high school. As a result, it was generally assumed, and expected, that I would be the section leader my senior year. I reacted to that expectation in two distinct ways:

1. I made a point of mastering the music we were playing, and

2. I made a point of observing the duties of the section leader.

A pair of simple questions present themselves:

1. Did I receive any extra training?

2. What actual training did I receive before I was appointed to the position?

By my senior year, I had been learning and playing my instrument for several years. In addition, I had been participating in sectional rehearsals for three years. In that time, I observed three section leaders as they led sectional rehearsals. What I knew about doing the job I learned from observing others doing the job. Of course, I supplemented that background with the lessons I learned while actually performing the required duties.

This is not an unusual pattern in a leadership journey. Organizations frequently promote from within. Individuals who are recognized for their qualities and achievements within the organization are recognized by being "rewarded" with an appointment to a leadership position.

Election to a Leadership Position

Once again, some additional background information on this leadership position: as with many other organizations, candidates for office in a local NEA chapter are nominated for the office by a nominating committee. Toward the end of my third year at the school, the nominating committee approached me to run for office for the following year. Given the structure of offices, the actual office I was nominated for was the office of "President-Elect". As is the case in many organizations, this position fills multiple roles:

1. The President-Elect serves as the "Vice President" and fills in for the President as needed.

2. The President-Elect provides a measure of continuity in the association leadership; once they complete their term as President-Elect, they automatically become the President for the next school year.

3. Once the President-Elect has moved up to and completed their term as President, they move to an advisory position of Immediate Past President for the following school year.

Part of the motivation for utilizing this succession scheme is to provide for continuity of leadership. As President-Elect, I was expected to attend leadership training and association meetings to find out the expectations of association leadership. In addition, the roles and responsibilities of each office were spelled out in the local association bylaws.

As a result, the year (actually a total of three years) passed with minimal complications. As President, I acted as the presiding officer at monthly membership meetings. I was able to pull together a budget for the year. I also delegated the responsibility for contract negotiations, selecting an experienced negotiator as chairman of the negotiation committee.

The natural question to ask is, "How did I prepare for this leadership position? I spent most of my first twenty post-collegiate years as a teacher--10 years at the secondary level and eight years at the collegiate level. (I also spent one year working in industry and one year in graduate school.) Of the 10 years I taught at the secondary level, nine years were at public school; the remaining year was in a private school. (The college I taught in was also a publicly funded institution.)

During my entire tenure in public education, both secondary and collegiate, I was a member of the local chapter of the National Education Association. I attended and participated in regularly scheduled meetings and worked on a number of ad hoc committees.

The result was a process of learning by immersion; I learned about the organization by observing it in action. At times, I also participated in meetings of the local chapters and other activities related to my memberships.

In addition to learning by immersion, I did receive some classroom-style training. This occurred after I was elected President of the local Education Association during my final secondary school position. This was a rather concentrated weekend seminar that included classes on the duties of the office, meeting procedures (such as Parliamentary Procedure), and other related topics.

All of the preparation was essentially one way; there were no tests and no feedback was provided. As a result, although I received training on leading the local Education Association, that training was generally oriented toward "what" rather than "how." I knew **what** roles, responsibilities, and duties were for the local President. Unfortunately, I was a bit shy on the **how**!

I did have a few advantages, however. As a member of the organization for several years, I was able to observe others in similar leadership positions and learn how the various offices operate by observing the officers in action. (Although I was a new officer, I was not an outsider to the organization!) Even with all the training and observation, I was learning on the job, in some cases learning from my own mistakes.

Lessons learned

These experiences highlight two common methods by which people learn and practice leadership: learning by observation and learning by experimentation. In my leadership journey, I have used both of these techniques; I have also relied on available leadership training and advice/mentoring to support my experience.

Ultimately, I believe that, while pre-knowledge and training are helpful, the most effective way to become a leader is to lead.

But what makes you step forward and accept the risks of leadership?

In the examples I have cited:

1. I was appointed by the band director, and

2. I was approached by the current leadership of the organization.

This gave me the impression that others, with positions of authority, were confident I could do the job. This was important as I had no experience in either position, but I was willing to take the risk of giving it a try.

In both cases, I had been an active member of the organization for multiple years. This enabled me to observe how others had handled the position and, based on those observations, I had a good handle on how to do the job.

The Feedback Loop

What was largely missing from the process was feedback. This was somewhat strange given that, as a teacher, a fairly large part of my job involved feedback. Every time I corrected a paper; I was looking for feedback. (Generally, I found it more effective to have the students correct their own homework as that provided some immediate feedback to the students.) I used that feedback to determine if the students understood the subject; indirectly, this also provided me with feedback relating to how well I was doing my job. For example, if I determined either the students didn't understand or I didn't get the point across, I could repeat the lesson.

Note the basic teaching cycle: instruction (in the classroom), practice (homework), feedback (checking the homework), and then applying the feedback to move forward. We can refer to this as the *feedback loop*.

Ultimately, as I assumed various leadership roles in life, the big missing element in the process was the *feedback loop*.

Lessons learned as a student

As noted in my entry in the *"Meet our Authors"* section at the back of this volume, I have earned a bachelor's degree and a master's degree in mathematics education. (At the time I decided to change my professional career path from teaching to software development, I was working toward a doctorate in mathematics.) As a result, I was very skilled and proficient in mathematics.

I did not, however, come upon those skills fully developed. Rather, I started out learning, and mastering, basic arithmetic. In the American school system of the time, this mastery was scheduled to last several years. As an early sign of my frustration with the system, I became so bored with the process of "relearning" things I had already mastered that I frequently neglected to complete routine homework assignments. After all, why must I do repetitive homework when I had already demonstrated I could do the actual work?

This led to two results. First, I nearly flunked my seventh-grade math class. Secondly, and much more importantly, I learned that, in real life, you may need to keep repeating the same things even after you have mastered the skill.

Throughout my academic life, I learned how to translate ideas that were demonstrated by the teacher in class into skills that, once I had mastered them, I could apply to solve new and more challenging problems.

Also importantly, in many endeavors in life, as in mountain climbing, you may reach the top, but you will need to start at the bottom of the next endeavor. Although you are starting something new, another mountain, you retain and utilize the skills and knowledge you have previously gained.

I found this was true in the study and mastery of mathematics. You do not start out studying Calculus or Abstract Algebra. Rather you start by learning and practicing basic arithmetic skills. You then progress through Algebra, Geometry,

Trigonometry, and on into more advanced mathematics starting with Calculus. As you progress into each new Mathematical field, you use and apply the knowledge and skills you have previously developed.

Along my mathematical journey, I learned some valuable everyday problem-solving skills. Perhaps most importantly, when faced with a new problem or situation, the two most critical questions to ask are "Where have I seen a similar problem in the past?" and "How is this problem different from other problems I have solved in the past?" Once you have identified the similarities and differences you will know where to start in order and what previously gained knowledge to solve the problem.

As I reflect on my mathematical journey, I realize that though academic work normally includes a feedback loop, that loop is frequently incomplete. The teacher provides feedback to the student via homework and test scores, but the feedback from the student to the teacher is rather sparse. Only rarely does a student contact a teacher personally regarding how things are progressing. For the feedback loop to work well it must be a two-way line of communication.

In addition to my undergraduate major in Mathematics education, I was required to have a "teaching minor" in another field of study. Normally, a person studying Mathematics would select a minor in either computer science or one of the sciences. Being a child of the sixties, I selected history as my "teaching minor". This allowed me to experience a second learning model: the lecture/test model. The contrast is rather stark.

In Mathematics, you attend classes and do homework. The classes tend to have a lecture/demonstration format. The homework allows the student to practice the material and provides a feedback loop between the teacher and the student. Periodic tests also feed the feedback loop

.

In History classes, the flow of information is generally one way: the teacher lectures, and the students listen and take notes. There tends to be minimal active interaction between the teacher and the students. There is also very minimal daily practice (homework) of the information presented in the class. The main feedback is via the tests.

Communication and Leadership

I should point out that, although this book is oriented around leadership, and the contributing authors all have experience with various types of leadership, there is more to being a leader than making and carrying out decisions, and presiding over an organization's meetings and working sessions.

A leader needs to be able to clearly communicate within the team. Being able to effectively communicate outside the team is also a crucial leadership skill. (For more information on communication and leadership see my chapter: *Communication and Leadership* in *Spotlight on the Art of Speaking by the Alternative Book Club.*

A Better Path to Leadership

Again, referring to my entry in the *"Meet our Authors"* section, I am a member of Toastmasters International, a membership organization that focuses on developing communication and leadership skills. Also noted in my bio, I have served in many leadership positions in that organization. This experience has led me to an improved path to becoming a leader.

First, my take on the Toastmasters learning model:

1. Toastmasters promotes an experiential learning process. Members prepare, practice, and receive feedback for each learning experience with a feedback loop.

2. Toastmasters promotes an incremental learning process. Members are encouraged to proceed in small steps and to apply lessons previously learned when taking the next step.

3. Toastmasters promotes a reflective learning process. Members are encouraged to apply lessons learned during each learning experience to help prepare for the next experience.

This learning model is applied to both leadership and communication goals.

I should note that although Toastmasters International has nearly 300,000 members located in 150 countries, the majority of its members work on the education program within a local Toastmasters club. Although club size varies, the average club has approximately 20 members. The members of each club are dedicated to improving their communication and leadership skills and, perhaps more importantly, are committed to helping their fellow club members in their communication and leadership journeys.

The bottom line? The Toastmaster's learning model is designed for and works best in a small group of individuals who want to improve their communication and leadership skills.

Applying this model

How do you utilize this learning model?

The first step is to set a goal for yourself. This doesn't have to be a SMART (Specific, Measurable, Achievable, Relevant, Time-bound) goal. You simply need to decide that you want to improve your leadership ability.

After you have made that decision, look for a group of people with similar goals who can assist you in meeting yours while you assist them in meeting theirs. This group may be a community-based group, such as a Toastmasters club, or a similar group sponsored by your employer. It may even be merely a friend or coworker who is willing to act as your mentor.

After you have decided to improve your leadership decision, you will need to develop a plan of action. Decide what areas of leadership you desire to improve. These can include leading a team, leading a project, leading a meeting, mentoring a co-worker, coaching a co-worker, or providing feedback to a co-worker. The possibilities are nearly endless.

The next step is to locate any materials you will need to work on the leadership skill you have decided to pursue. These may be obtained from any of several sources including the internet, your local library, or a local bookstore.

The rest of your journey involves the feedback loop: prepare, perform, receive feedback, apply the feedback, and repeat.

Conclusion

If you take the time and prepare, you can develop into a leader. All that is required is some planning and practice. Put together a team to assist in your journey. Be sure to include a robust feedback mechanism.

Reflection Questions

1. What leadership positions have you held in the recent past?

2. For each of these positions, consider

a. How were you selected for the position?

b. How did you prepare for the position?

c. Looking back, what changes would you make to better prepare for the position?

5

Leading with Humility; Following with Courage

By: Janel Asche

Do nothing out of selfish ambition or vain
conceit. Rather, in humility value others above
yourselves.
                                        ~ Philippians 2:3-4

Mutual Need, Mutual Benefit

Where would our world be with no leaders, no leaders at all?
Everyone would be operating independently on tasks of limited
scope and perhaps benefiting only themselves. Yes, it's likely
there was one person who developed the first wheel, arrowhead,
or woven basket, but until that person led others to copy and
enhance those devices, there was no widespread benefit.

Now, suppose there were no followers. Individuals would be trying to accomplish some tasks too large for just themselves but getting nowhere, because no one would help. In the end, as in the world without leaders, everyone would be doomed to a very small existence.

Leaders and followers are mutually required. Only with both can the greatest projects succeed. Only with both can the world thrive. Both have great value and purpose, but they are not usually appreciated to the same degree.

In our society, leaders are often looked at as heroes. Certain presidents, great generals, courageous advocates, and even some corporate CEOs are considered great leaders who rescued some segment of the population. Students often think of their teachers, principals, and superintendents as heroes who guided them through to success. We tend to consider leaders to be courageous, fearless, and self-assured. In contrast, followers are often viewed as sheep, or worse as lemmings, acting only in accordance with what the leader says as if trapped in a childhood game. Simon says, "Tote that barge." "Now, lift that bale." "You're out; Simon didn't say so." Those are the stereotypes: courageous leaders and humble followers. Wait, though. Is that the way it really is? Is that the way it should be? Is that the way that works best?

Leaders as Courageous Heroes, or Not

Indeed, many leaders are courageous heroes. In reality, though, leaders are not always that courageous. They might not have even been interested in the position. Instead, leadership was foisted upon them due to circumstances beyond their control. There were no volunteers, so they were "voluntold" to take the lead. There was no one else with the skills to plan the escape, battle, or surprise party. There was no one else with the vision to guide the production of an opera, art show, or time machine. What if the leader has absolutely no experience in leading nor knowledge relevant to the project at hand?

A few decades ago, I found myself in just that situation; no experience and no knowledge, leading part of a large project in its early stages. They had divvied out lead assignments in a rather random way. It was as if, when no one was expressly an expert on that part of the system, they pulled a name out of a hat. I was a mere babe in that job, barely knowing even a bite-sized piece of my department's slice of the system pie. The project itself was still very new with minimal system descriptions or requirements.

For example, one critical and complex part of the project had a requirements document just one and one-half pages long that might as well have been one sentence: "The system should work just like today, but with entirely different input and significantly different expected results." Luckily, I did not end up with that part of the project. Instead, the part I was given was for an entirely new function that involved interactive screens that would require software languages I did not know. Though I tried to courageously embrace the role, I was far too new and I was the only software developer assigned to the group of very experienced business analysts. I felt (and was) inadequate for the task.

After several meetings about the query system to be developed, the main thing we accomplished was finding a better acronym than the proposed "BURP," a name so meaningful I've forgotten exactly what the letters stood for; Browse, Update, Replace, Purge, maybe? Thankfully, management finally concluded that random assignment was not the way to go.

On the other hand, one of the other sub-projects assigned to me was truly in my slice of the system pie. However, though they considered me expert enough to lead the effort to overhaul that part of the system, it was something I had barely tasted. I'd sampled a crumb of the crust, at best. That put me in good company. No one then on the team had tasted more of it than I had. It was considered a black box. In other words, the code worked, but no one then on the team could say how or why it worked. It performed an essential part of our system, but the writers were long gone, the code was convoluted, the documentation—if any had ever been produced—was lost to the ages, but the black box functioned well. In the end, "If it ain't broke, don't fix it" meant if it worked, we had neither time nor budget to spend analyzing and documenting that black box. Our process for using the box was to find some similar usage, make the necessary adjustments for several bits of input data, then call the black box to do the magic needed. The guiding mantra was, "It works. No one knows how or why it works. Don't touch it."

Rumor had it the project lead assigned me that bit specifically because they did not want to touch it. The supposition was the lead had fully internalized the mantra and figured if someone had to struggle and fail, it would be less embarrassing if it were the newbie.

Again, I initially found myself feeling very inadequate. How could I lead this one any better than BURP? At least this time, I knew where to look and knew the programming language being used. With that, I felt more courageous and capable than I did with BURP. Once I delved into the program, I discovered many interesting things. The black box code was written as generically as possible to cover every type of relevant data sent to it and every possible result.

Of course, the problem with such good intentions is the system invariably grows enough in size and complexity that generics no longer cover every flavor of input and output required. Once I was given enough time to thoroughly analyze and digest that part of the system, I discovered all the intricacies, creative forethought, and missed predictions. I discovered the data names being used in the black box were used nowhere else and were completely misleading. It was the mark of a good intention that was abandoned but had become entrenched enough it was easier to leave the data names in place than to change the system to be less confusing. At times, it seemed confusion was the goal.

When I was able to understand and explain in detail how that subsystem worked, I could easily lead discussions on the topic. I could describe why something went amiss, what options were available to correct the problem, and even document the black box in a way all could understand. I became the subject matter expert on that slice of a slice. The customers and fellow technical analysts all came to me for advice on the matter. They were certain I knew more than they did and would have their answers or, at least, be able to guide them to what they needed. Still, I knew enough to know I did not know enough to say I knew it all. That self-awareness kept me humble enough to avoid being an annoying know-it-all. Fortunately, it's not necessary to know everything to lead.

How much does the leader need to know? From my experience, I would say the leader needs to know enough about the system to be able to spot when something is clearly wrong. They need to be able to correctly identify who knows the most about the system and who's just guessing or "faking it 'til they make it." In BURP, I had no idea who knew even where to start. I was trying to bake a pumpkin pie in a gas oven without knowing how to—even being afraid to—light the pilot. It was just a mushy mess in a flimsy aluminum pie tin. Conversely, in the black box project, not only was I fully capable of getting the pilot lit, I knew how to check and repair the gas line, how to maintain the perfect temperature, and how to test for impeccable results. That sturdy ceramic pie plate held a well-structured, sweet finish. Courage, with the strong footing in knowledge, made the leadership experience more productive, more successful, and much more pleasant.

Followers as Humble Sheep

To be certain, there are blind followers of any leader, no matter how corrupt, unknowledgeable, or incompetent that leader may be. Blind followers with unquestioning obedience may seem efficient, but is it most effective? Humble sheep resist challenging authority. Even when they have ideas for a better solution, they keep quiet. They don't want to rock the boat. They devalue their thoughts; they are not the leaders, so they deem their thoughts to be unworthy, except where they coincide with those of their leader. In such an environment, individual expertise and creativity can be wasted.

For instance, I was once on a project led by someone outside of my slice of the system. In a meeting with customers, the lead was incorrectly describing the slice-of-a-slice I had lived and breathed for a couple of years by then. Although, I tried to correct their statements, I was too intimidated to force the issue, my word against that of one of the star technical leads. I was indeed correct, but I allowed myself to be convinced I was not. I devalued my thoughts as mere opinions rather than facts. I was being a humble follower, not the courageous one I needed to be. In that way, my expertise was wasted in the discussion. I kept having to correct and disprove the leader's misstatements while I explained and proved all of my recommendations. That ended up unnecessarily prolonging the search for the solution because the leader's description was what got lodged in the team members' memories.

Ignoring creativity is as much of a waste as denying expertise. I remember in one of our "soft-skills" (non-technical) training classes we were divided into groups of five. Then, we were tasked with composing a poem on a supplied topic. We were to work together, not individually, to come up with a poem in ten minutes. By "time's up," we had an incredibly short stanza worthy of any fourth-grader. The second half of the experiment was to take ten minutes to come up with a poem on our own. Writing poetry being one of my strengths, I had a consistently metered, evocative poem of multiple stanzas at the end of those ten minutes. When we worked independently, several of us exhibited much more creativity and skill than we did as a group. Left to our own devices, we completed much longer and more interesting poems. The point was creative tasks are often better accomplished when team members are allowed to work on their own and then bring their ideas back to the group. Why? Even in the typical brain-storming session, where there is not supposed to be any judgment passed on any idea until the post-storm evaluation, individuals can still feel intimidated, as I did under the leadership of that star technical lead.

I came to realize following as humble sheep rather than speaking up does not always bring the best result. I would hazard a guess that it seldom does. Unless your team is very small, chances are there are followers with varied, valuable ideas. They may be clearly better in their own right, or they may stimulate alternative ideas from others. It takes courage to share new ideas and courage to act on them, but sometimes courage is in short supply.

Value of Courage

I have never considered myself very courageous, though there are some who consider me to be so. I often wish I were what they believed. I can think of many areas of my life that would be changed if only I were a bit braver than I am. For example, I have a children's book, written decades ago, wasting away in a digital file. I wrote it and considered trying to get it published. After receiving encouragement from family, friends, a couple of innocent bystanders, and my kindergartner's entire class, I did some research on what to do to send it to publishers or if I needed an agent, etc. Yet, I never sent anything anywhere because I feared the inevitable rejection letters. Who knows? I could have become a successful children's author with dozens of books to my name. Will I ever get it published? Maybe, hopefully, if I can summon up the courage (and the currency) to do so, because courage drives action, and action brings change.

Value of Courage in a Follower

I heard a speech once, given by a woman who stood up during an all-employee corporate meeting and challenged the panel of corporate heads on the fact that virtually all the company's leaders were Caucasian men. The corporate head leading the meeting had asked if there were any questions. The woman stood up, took the microphone and bravely spoke out about the lack of diversity, insisting on a response. I honestly cannot see myself doing anything like that. I admire her courage and that of all those who dare to speak out. They are the ones that make change happen. Followers with that level of courage become leaders themselves, even if they continue to serve the existing authority.

Value of Humility

Courage is clearly a valuable commodity, but there is value in humility, too, no matter who you are and in what position. Humble people are more approachable. They are more relatable and more willing to listen to others. They realize the world is not all about themselves. They fully recognize the value of those around them. They recognize talent, effort, and better ideas and understand they may not have any of the three. They recognize truth and accept it, no matter how much it conflicts with their existing worldview or preferences. Had that star technical lead been leading with humility, they would have eagerly sought and accepted my expertise, opinions, and ideas. As it was, intentionally or not, I was stifled, and the project progress was stymied.

Value of Humility in a Leader

Can one be courageous and humble at the same time? Certainly! Some of our greatest world leaders have optimized the balance. Franklin Delano Roosevelt, Martin Luther King, Jr., Harry S. Truman, and Steve Jobs, for example, all relied heavily on not being the smartest person in the room. Great leaders recognize their weaknesses, surround themselves with experts and listen to their advice. Then, barring good reason not to, the leaders act on that expert advice. The key is knowing what you know, knowing what you need, and knowing who can help. With BURP, I had three strikes against me. Though I knew what I knew, that

111

knowledge was essentially nothing. I did not know enough to even know what I needed. Without that knowledge, I had no idea who might help with answers. It was less leading with humility than it was leading with humiliation.

Wait! Is it possible to be humble yet claim humility? Isn't declaring yourself humble oxymoronic? Surely, claiming you are humble negates the idea that you truly are, unless you are speaking of being of humble origin, maybe born in poverty. Looking at a list of synonyms for "humble," they hardly describe someone likely to lead: meek, lowly, submissive, deferential, sycophantic, and mim. Raise your hand if you knew "mim" means demure. My hand was down. Did it take some humility to admit you did not know that word? Yes. It did. My answer is this: you do not really need to be overly humble to lead with humility. You just need to be able to see beyond yourself. You need to see the value of others and the knowledge beyond your own. You can be self-assured and confident, yet lead with humility. That blend of traits can inspire dedication among followers, resulting in greater team cohesion.

Success of the Team

I was far more successful in a project for Toastmasters, a volunteer speaking and leadership group I joined. For the year-end district celebration, the district director was in charge of the theme, venue, and agenda. I handled everything else for the event as my High Performance Leadership (HPL) project.

The HPL is one of the most challenging steps toward Toastmasters' highest-level achievement award, Distinguished Toastmaster (DTM). It requires organization and leadership of multiple teams toward a single sizeable goal. I was as much of a neophyte as I was for BURP, but I had a much better idea of what I needed to do, what I knew, what I needed, and who could help. I needed to organize food, decorations, photographers, activities and entertainment. I needed invitations, promotions, reminders, and response tracking. I also needed to handle some logistics. Clearly, it was too much for just one person. To be a leader, I needed to find some followers. I needed to break down the event into manageable chunks and find a leader for each chunk. They, in turn, would find followers to take on a tidbit each.

Some helpers were easier to find than others. Ann, the district public relations manager (DPRM) was the ideal choice to handle invitations and all necessary follow-ups. She and I worked together and separately to come up with some engaging communications with potential attendees and potential helpers. "Year-end Round-up" was the theme. We put on our ten-gallon thinking hats to make everything sound as cowboy western as we could. People were chomping at the bit to mosey over to the park and belly up to the food bar. In fact, considerably more district members signed up to attend that year's celebration compared to the past. "We done a durn fine job, we did!"

My two HPL guidance committee members also volunteered; Beth for set-up and Carol for take-down. I asked my extremely creative and artistic club mentor, Debbie, to take on the decorations. She and the rest of the set-up committee made my vision of an old-time country picnic come to life. Another part of my vision was to include some country music in the fun. My daughter, Allison, a talented hoofer, accepted my challenge to lead line dancing, all decked out in country duds. One district member, Ethan, came highly recommended to manage the sound system on the park basketball-court dance floor. He worked with my daughter on the perfect playlist. The rest of the volunteers were strangers to me, volunteering in response to Ann's promotion emails. The two largest committees were for food and activities. The former was made up of a mix of members from various clubs. The latter was primarily handled by one tight-knit club.

As the project progressed, I communicated regularly with the committee chairs, fielding questions, tracking down answers, and checking on status. Sometimes, it felt like I got a dozen emails and twenty text messages every day from my committee leaders. I was determined not to micromanage or take over completely. A large part of the HPL learning experience was to choose your teams, give them guidance, and trust them to make it happen while maintaining communication and support. However, the larger the committee, the more difficult it can be to reach a decision. I found I needed to offer greater guidance to the two largest groups of volunteers. In both cases, they had more ideas than final decisions, so I helped them to pick and choose and commit to a final plan. In the end, we had both a fabulous feast and a marvelous array of activities ranging from printed ice-breaker games to a beanbag toss and a giant take on a classic old-fashioned game—marbles. Instead of a string ring, there was a rope one. Instead of shooting tiny glass orbs, basketballs were the shooters while the ring held a variety of smaller spheres.

There was feasting and fun for hours; members chatting, laughing, playing, and dancing. Allison coaxed more and more shy souls out onto the dance court, lines of folks stomping in rhythm. When things finally died down, Carol's take-down crew made quick work of the clean-up. The truly fantastic part of it all was that even leading the celebration, I was able to enjoy it, too. That's the best part about learning to break a project down—divide it up, delegate, and communicate. We managed to have all the pieces worked out ahead of time so the event ran smoothly, giving each of us the chance to enjoy the fun.

After the event, I received an email of glowing appreciation for the round-up. I passed the message on to the dozens of celebration team members, adding my own effusive congratulations and thanks for their extremely successful efforts. They all deserved individual callouts with specific recognition for their work. I sent the email to the group with a courtesy copy to the district director so she could see how many contributed to the event and in what way. I wanted to be sure they all understood how meaningfully they affected the festivities. As with humility, the value of gratitude in leadership cannot be overstated.

I'm glad I was brave enough to take on the project, but I'm happiest that I led with enough humility to inspire courage from our committee leaders. They would come to me with suggestions, because they had the courage to come forward with their thoughts. Though they did not always match my vision, some were definitely better ideas. I embraced those ideas and encouraged more. Was that always easy? No, admittedly it was not. Sometimes my gut wanted my first response to be a firm no. However, I deliberately deliberated to quiet my gut and decided nothing without considering consequences. The outcome was better than I could have hoped, all because of the right combination of humility and courage.

Missing the Mark—Almost

Now, you might think that after such a successful leadership experience, I had everything down pat. You might think so, but that was not the case. The next time I was in charge of food for a Toastmasters event ultimately succeeded, but there were bumps that could have spoiled it all—bumps that could have been avoided. This time, I was in charge of just the food for the district contest, but for two days, not just five hours. That should definitely have been easier than what I needed to do for the round-up, right? Again, the venue was already secured and the agenda was on the organizer's plate, not mine. Initially, food direction was minimal, but it became very specific, with a bit of overkill in some aspects—we ended up with water and coffee enough for at least four times as many attendees, and that was cut down considerably from the detailed list I was given.

There was early debate on what would be served for supper the first day and for lunch the second day. The final decisions were evening pizza and boxed lunches from a highly-recommended sandwich chain restaurant. I rounded up volunteers and broke down the tasks like I should. This time, for a multi-day event, I had to also set a larger-scale timeline. We needed everyone to get their part of the meals where they needed to be, when. We also had to work around the speeches presented without being disruptive. If you are a Toastmasters member, you are familiar with the minute-by-minute agenda for every club meeting. The

117

district conference is nearly as strictly scheduled, making prompt food arrival and set up essential.

I had a detailed spreadsheet of who was assigned which task, along with their contact information and timeline. What a nicely organized thing to do! Unfortunately, I forgot my hardcopy at home and could not access the file via my phone. Our pizza volunteer, Fred, emailed me the day before the conference to let me know he would be in a town 200 miles away but assured me the pizzas would be picked up and on site as scheduled. It made me a bit nervous, but I trusted him. Fred had very specific orders for what to get. However, when he placed the order, the 16" pizza size designated was no longer sold. Fred did not have my phone number to call for advice, so he thought on his feet and upsized the pies. Thankfully, Fred got the goods to the venue as scheduled, but upsizing the order meant we ended up with a great surplus of pizza. Of course, according to most people I know, there's really no such thing as too much pizza.

The next morning, as we waited for the doughnut arrival, I got a bit jittery and decided to check to see if Greg, our pastry volunteer, was on his way. I discovered, though, I did not have more than his email address. He had been a bit of a last-minute addition to the volunteer list, and I failed to get his phone number on my spreadsheet. Instead, I emailed him to check his progress, knowing full well that, if he was like me, he would likely not even see the message until much later. Fortunately, he was not like me and actually responded within ten minutes, letting me know he was on his way. Once again, a little bump cleared with ease. The big bump would come next.

For lunch, day two, we had approximately forty attendees to feed. Jimmy, a Toastmaster I had met and knew by reputation to be very responsible, volunteered to handle the boxed lunches. We had already determined what kinds of sandwiches and salads to order. After discovering requests for more than twenty lunches required ordering by 3:00 pm the day before the event, I emailed the policy to Jimmy. Thankfully, Hannah, one of the district leaders, checked in with me to make sure we would have food for the masses. When I caught up with Jimmy, though, to see if he had placed the order, he had missed the message about needing to order the day before.

He immediately called the nearest of the chain restaurant locations and tried to place the order. They essentially laughed in his face, reciting their policy to him. Jimmy, Hannah, and I confabbed to come up with a solution. What if we ordered half the sandwiches from each of two locations? That sounded like a solid plan, until he tried to place the half-order at the first store. They promptly hung up on him! I'm not sure how the manager felt about losing the sizeable sale, but the second store happily took our order and our money. We had to rearrange pick-up duties, but the meals were done, delicious and delivered right on time.

I learned a few lessons from that experience. Always, always, always have everyone's complete contact information, phone and email, at hand. Be sure to have a hardcopy and a copy on your phone in a location that does not require internet access to reference. What's more, be sure all your volunteers have your phone number and email address, too. Also, be sure to follow up emails with a more immediate form of communication—phone call or text message—whether or not your email got a response and no matter how much you trust the person involved. There's always potential for a miss.

If a miss occurs, take ownership of it and work out a solution as quickly as possible. Assignment of blame would only have slowed progress toward a solution and would have made everyone feel worse. Working together for success relieves the tension of the situation by actively showing support. It disentangles the negativity strangling all creativity, allowing positive thoughts for problem resolution. Finally, I learned that anything that looks like a success is a success. In other words, even if you feel like you failed in multiple ways, anyone who doesn't see the madly paddling feet under the water will think you're swimming along effortlessly.

Conclusion

Leaders and followers are mutually required. Their existence defines each other. From the earliest days of invention, community, and warfare, leaders led the way to change, but followers did a great deal of the work. Followers must also have been responsible for many of the ideas that led to improvements in processes and products along the way. It requires humility in leadership to be open to those ideas and courage in followers to make those ideas known. Approaching leadership with humility, admitting you do not have all the answers, opens you up to valuable advice and new perspectives. Approaching followership with courage enables you to contribute to and inspire the best solutions and broaden the leader's perceptions. Where humble leaders and courageous followers converge, teamwork is maximized. Lead with humility, follow with courage, and make great things can happen.

Reflection Questions

1. What is your leadership style? Do you lead with humility

2. In what situation have you been a courageous follower?

3. When have you followed like a humble sheep? Did you follow despite misgivings?

4. How would your life change if you were more courageous?

5. What do you consider the most important trait of a leader?

6. What world leader do you most respect? Why?

7. What leader in your personal, work, social, or religious community do you most respect?

8. Should leaders always be open to listening to followers?

6

Who? Me? A Leader?

By: Christine Jones

"The hardest person you will ever have to lead is yourself."

~Bill George

What is the Meaning of Leadership?

Is leadership just being bossy? Is it delegating duties? Is it attending a bunch of meetings? Is it looking important? Is it making promises that you do not really intend to keep? Is it creating the schedule for your employees? Is it ordering supplies and then paying for them? Is it sitting in your corner office watching the world go by? Does it allow you to control others?

When I looked up "leader" in my Merriam-Webster dictionary, I found that it is, in fact, someone who guides or has commanding authority. Those both sound like opposing definitions to me! One sounds like a mother or father figure who is nurturing their employees like their children. The other sounds like a military officer that barks orders all day. In reality, a leader has to have the authority to make crucial decisions that will keep everyone moving forward. (As we will learn later in this chapter, someone who tries to control another person is not leading.) I feel that both traits are essential to a good leader. The trick comes in knowing how much of which definition to employ at any given time. Let's see how these definitions have impacted my leadership.

Is It a Pass/Fail Situation?

Obviously, leaders can fail. Using football coaches as an example, if a coach does not lead the team to a winning season, they are very likely to lose their job. In business, there could be a job loss depending on the situation. There may be a reprimand or it is just chalked up to a learning opportunity. As a leader in a volunteer organization, I led a club for a year. This club, being part of an international organization, had ten goals that allowed the club to earn points for levels of achievement. The highest achievement is Distinguished which means "made conspicuous by excellence," according to dictionary.com. It is a challenge to see how many clubs around the world can earn the highest distinguished status of completing all ten goals. While we had a fun year, I was not able to take the club to a distinguished status of achieving those specified goals. While I completed the required year of service toward my personal goal, I did feel like

I had failed to take the club to a new level of growth. I did learn that if the entire club is not working toward the same goals, that list of ten specified goals can never be reached. I did find that our club is successful at maintaining our club goals of being a fun and nurturing environment. With that moment of learning being my takeaway from the experience, I was thankful for the opportunity to learn and serve.

That leaves me to say that success depends on <u>your</u> specific leadership situation. You can pass on parts of the experience and fail on others. What matters is that you take the opportunity to learn. A volunteer-led organization can be a great place to develop your skills. Look at several other chapters in this collection to see what experiences they have had.

What Makes Me Qualified?

Unlike some of the others writing in this book, I have never felt qualified to lead. Just the thought of taking a leadership position, even a club officer as a volunteer, brought about sweaty palms, a racing heart, and the desire to flee as quickly as possible.

I managed to avoid being a leader during my professional life. As an introvert, I was content to quietly do my job under the leadership of a woman who demonstrated the nurturing as defined above. It was not her fault that we went through the stress of a company that downsized us out of our jobs.

125

She was such a refreshing leader after having endured a leader who thought women didn't belong in the workplace He was very controlling of every moment of my day and hated when I did not kowtow to his demands that I fetch his coffee. My job was as a computer auditor, not a gopher. He stressed me to the point that it was impacting my health and my marriage. I was bottling up my issues instead of talking to my husband about them. Here is just one example: In one meeting with a Vice President of a division, as the meeting began, my boss commented, "She belongs home, barefoot and pregnant." I was there to present my report on an audit finding that was creating financial loss to a customer. My controlling boss decided that I had been there long enough and he would finish the presentation.

While the other department head rolled his eyes and shook his head, my boss sent me out of the meeting so he could "handle the audit report presentation on his own." What he failed to cover was a significant financial risk that I had identified in my research. The programmer was skimming a customer. I found it. The boss did not report it to the VP who could deal with it. As a result of my boss sugar-coating my report, the Vice President of the division did not fully read my report. No action had been taken. It took the client who suffered financial loss to bring the issue to light. The person responsible was arrested and the issue was cleaned up by another reliable employee. The company was

126

fortunate that the client was able to recoup their losses that should have been avoided or at least minimized.

After enduring a controlling boss and benefitting from a nurturing boss, I did find another leadership position. Parenthood! The pay has been lousy but the benefits and rewards are absolutely amazing! I took on the leadership of raising two wonderful human beings. Again, I did not necessarily feel qualified yet I did have good role models of parents. They not only took on the roles of grandparents, they were my mentors.

I was fortunate to still have a grandmother of my own whom I asked for advice. Her advice became my mantra when I was struggling with my ability to be a good parent. I asked, "What advice do you have for me?" She said, "They will teach you everything you need to know." She was right! My kids are still an important part of my life as are their spouses and the three grandkids that have been added to the family.

Even though you do not feel qualified to take on a leadership role, you might just surprise yourself. Dig deep inside and seize a leadership opportunity. No matter what type of leader you have, you can learn along the way. That is why we are sharing our stories in this book! We want you to learn from our experiences. We are writing about the realities that you need to know about as you navigate your path of leadership and life in general.

You need to start with a bit of confidence.

What Makes Me Confident?

Being an introvert, my confidence can be hard to find. I have to work through those sweaty palms, a racing heartbeat, and that desire to flee. It has taken me years of developing and practicing some skills that helped make me more confident.

Breathing

The first skill I practice is just breathing. Take a minute and do a bit of breathing for yourself.

Inhale deeply, filling your lungs as full as possible to a count of five.

Now, exhale slowly to a count of ten.

Repeat three times.

How much calmer do you feel now? Are you clearer-minded? Can you better identify what is stressing you? When you can identify your stressors, you can control them better and thereby increase your self-confidence. (I also notice that after I take a few minutes to breathe, my palms are often less sweaty even though I am still thinking about fleeing!)

Joining Toastmasters

Joining Toastmasters International has been a wonderful opportunity for me to build my self-confidence. I definitely am now better able to tell controlling people that I am not going to be controlled by them.

I was confronted by a gentleman who did not like the fact that I turned the lights off as usual when the majority of the group was leaving the room following a meeting one day. He was still engaged in conversation with two ladies "about how we do things in our club." Since we limit our time in the community space we use, we do not usually tarry long which meant I anticipated he would be also leaving shortly. The lights being off did not make the room dark by any means so it was absolutely not a safety issue. As we prepared to begin the next meeting, I was surprised by him literally getting in my face and talking loud enough for most of the room to hear his words. "You do not turn the lights off when I am still in the room. It was an interruption to our meeting. I will let you know when you can turn them off." I was biting my tongue so hard to keep from laughing in his face. (The other boss would have me cowering in fear. No more.) I did say, "You do not control me. I do not work for you so you do not have controlling authority over me."

Yes, I was having flashbacks to that controlling boss. No, he was not happy with my comments.

What did I do? I made the best of the meeting and was glad to have to leave right after for another appointment. I was <u>not</u> ready to have any further contact with him. When I got home, I sat down to write out my thoughts and reactions. Since we give evaluations in response to speeches, I took that approach as I made my notes. What he did, followed by what he would be better doing and, how he made me feel by his actions. After an hour of making notes, I shut the computer off and walked away to do something else for a while. Then, since my husband had been there, I did share my notes with him to get his opinion about what I should do next. We agreed that I needed to talk to my mentor. This man helped me from the day I joined the club to get acclimated to "how we do things" and has been a sounding board for many of my projects. I did send him my notes and specified that they not be sent on to the other man. He agreed. He also agreed with what I had put in my notes. He had been across the room at the time but heard every word that was spoken. He talked me out of quitting that day and then told me his plan. Without showing the other man the document I created, he was going to sit him down to remind him that we are not in a controlling environment and encourage him to rein in his behavior.

At the moment, he has toned his behavior down a notch at least towards me. We will see how long this lasts.

How do I feel? I am still feeling a bit uncomfortable around him. It is a bit like waiting for "the other shoe to drop." Knowing that others are aware of what happened, helps keep me feeling safe and wanted. While he has not apologized, he has been civil to me. (I do not feel like controlling people are generous with apologies so I will not hold my breath waiting for one.) I will keep taking our encounters one at a time. I am just quite alert to doing my best not to trigger him into thinking he needs to take control of any situation. It is a bit like walking on eggshells yet I do not want to give up a group that I have enjoyed for many years. It becomes a place where <u>he</u> can hopefully learn better leadership skills as a result of our interactions. While it may be uncomfortable for me, I do see this as an opportunity to help teach better skills to someone else.

It is a good training ground!

What Makes One Trained?

Have you ever wondered what makes anyone trained? I have. I remember the days of submitting resumes along with job applications as I was about to graduate college.

Businesses wanted people with experience but how are you supposed to get experience when you are just graduating from your schooling phase of life? You think you have the training you need yet experience seems to be a totally different element. Your education may have given you knowledge while life experiences are what really train you. After all, training is where you practice applying your knowledge to a given situation. Until you are repeatedly in actual situations, it is difficult to claim that you are sufficiently trained. It took several applications and rejections to find a job that was willing to give me the experience of using my skills.

Experience is not learned in a book. It is a process of personal encounters and observation according to my dictionary. That sounds like another word for life! Every day we get the opportunity to experience new events. How we use and react to them is what builds our experience.

When I finally left the business world for the world of parenting, I did not feel trained even though I had life experience babysitting. Yes, it was valuable knowledge, yet when you have your own baby to care for, those first days are a crash course of training! It can be quite stressful.

Training is not only knowledge. Training includes practical experiences. Does stress always play a part in training? While a significant part of leadership can be stress-related, it should not be the only emotion.

What Part Do Emotions Play?

As noted during that crash course phase of parenting, stress can run rampant. Are you feeding the baby the right way? Are they eating enough? How often do diapers need to be changed? Am I even using the right kind of diaper? When can I get some sleep? When did I eat last? When did I last get a shower? Is the room too hot or too cold? Who does this baby most resemble? Does the baby even like me? This repeats with each child.

Did you note that there are many emotions involved in those few questions? No matter what your scenario might be, I am sure you can make a list of similar questions that will include many emotions. You will note fear and excitement along with anxiety among them. How you use those emotions will impact your leadership abilities whether you are parenting or leading in the office. If you show an overabundance of any emotion, your leadership ability may lose credibility. People see you as out of control rather than seeing you as one who uses your emotions to propel yourself to solve problems.

Rather than being so afraid to take action that you are paralyzed, take time to breathe. Then, start making a list of options to solve your problem(s). Let's continue with the new baby challenges. That baby needs you to lead them by fulfilling their every essential need. When you exude fear, the baby will pick up on this emotion by becoming afraid, too. Then, you both will end up in a mess of tears and desperately needing to breathe! Starting with calming breaths followed by a good plan will leave everyone happy and emotions under control. Do not forget that a key option for solving any problem is asking for help. You are never required to do everything on your own.

I know. I know. You are thinking that you are not a leader if you cannot do everything yourself. Let's spend some time on that topic.

How Do Other Leaders Impact My Ability to Lead?

While in Toastmasters, I needed to do a project that demonstrated my ability to lead. My intended project was to update a list of trained people for another person who needed to complete their files for the next speech contest season. As a leader to me, he was to introduce me and the planned project to the clubs grouped into what we call a district. He kept putting off that introduction. The time window in which I needed to work was rapidly closing. I finally sent out an email to everyone, telling them what I was doing, who it was for, and asking for their response that would allow me to update the file. While I got many valuable responses, I got less than expected. When I reached out to those who did not respond to the first email, I got responses that indicated since they did not know me, they wanted no part in the process. Needless to say, his list still was not as updated as he wanted. I was frustrated but did my best to complete the task.

It was a different leadership experience than that controlling leader I mentioned earlier in this chapter. I want to spend a few moments here to complete the story of what happened after his remarks about my belonging at home.

My controlling boss? He reamed me out back in our offices as well as complained to our department head. The result? Nothing was done to deal with the controller. My next employee review included a note that I was an "uncooperative employee." In time, he made my work environment so miserable that I no longer felt safe alone in a room with him. (These days, I would have grounds for a lawsuit against him.) When it happened, I was told by Personnel that it was just "the boss being in control." I would have to endure it or go find another job. It took a toll on me both mentally and physically. With no support from the company, I sought employment elsewhere.

A peer at another company assisted me by connecting me with his boss. She could not wait for me to escape from that unpleasant environment! It was such a pleasant change. She found me to be a very cooperative and capable employee. The company was very supportive of their employees which was quite refreshing. A better environment along with medical care and counseling were essential to restoring my health.

My point? Being a controlling leader can cost you quality employees. These days there could also be legal and financial ramifications.

Leading an organization vs. leading in other environments

Leading a club may not be exactly like leading an organization or a project. There are similarities. You still have people that you are guiding to accomplish a goal. In a company, you have more employees yet it boils down to how you lead. As long as everyone is focused on achieving the same goal, the number of people involved matters only regarding how much work needs to be done. Sufficient staffing is the key. You have to let the employees do the work. You need to support and encourage them. You need to establish realistic goals. Since I have never led in a business environment, let me share an environment where I have more knowledge. You can decide if leading a business is similar. (I believe there are many similarities.)

Look at the structure of a family. As a parent, your family is the staff that you lead. No matter the size of your family, each member still will have chores to complete as they learn life skills and work toward family goals such as being positive contributors to society.

It all has a purpose

Leaders are essential to helping to achieve goals. Whether you are in an organization, a corporation, or even a family, it takes leadership to achieve goals. Organizational and corporate goals with a purpose trending toward success plans and being profitable. Family goals have a different purpose.

In a family, raising children who are assets to society should be a realistic goal. In my opinion, the purpose of parenting is to guide children as they learn right from wrong and develop the talents and skills that can carry them through life. Along the way, parents are leaders as they work through the daily challenges of food, laundry, employment, children's activities, friendships, and whatever else you can think of! This form of leadership is role modeling. While you use words to express instructions, actions can speak louder than words. Children are masters at learning by imitation. We must demonstrate good leadership by making sure we are also taking good care of our health.

Future leaders come from family-type environments that have a common purpose of creating future leaders. Whether biological, adopted, fostered, or orphaned, family environments are where leadership skills are often developed.

We do not lead the same!

If the family environment is where leadership skills are developed, why are there differing leadership styles?

Have you looked at how many different ways people parent? From "helicopter parents" who want to constantly monitor every move of their child to "my kid can do no wrong" parenting styles, parents do not lead the same. If parents do not parent the same, the leaders that come from these environments will never lead the same.

After all, leading can be like parenting if you think about it. Look at your leadership style. How much does it resemble how you were parented? Does your style resemble how you parent? Are you raising your children differently than how you were raised? Please tell me you use a style sensitive to others rather than being a control freak.

Is working with peers a form of leadership?

Quilters working as a group

One of my hobbies is making quilt tops for a service group at my church. This is an older group of ladies who enjoy giving quilts to those in need. Fabric is donated at a rate that keeps us well-supplied. The church does fund some of the rest of our supplies such as the batting that goes between the quilt top and back layers as quilts are assembled. What a joy it is to watch the ladies working as a group. Once a top is created, ladies pick through the fabric supply to help create an appropriate back. Ladies then create what is called the sandwich where the front, batting, and back are carefully aligned then pinned together. Other ladies are stationed at sewing machines ready to sew the quilt into being. Then, the quilt is passed to still other ladies who tie knots through the layers of the quilt. This step is important to keep the layers from shifting during use. The knots also add character to the quilt.

What we have found is that most of the ladies have a task that they prefer. It takes all of us working together to achieve the common goal of creating quilts to serve others. Do we have a leader? There are two ladies that we look to for direction when we have questions. They are not afraid to discuss and then share how we proceed. They welcome input from anyone who has suggestions. They know each other well enough that even if the other is not available, they are consistently united in our directions. They often remind us that there is more than one way to achieve our goal of serving others by creating quilts. Every lady feels valued and enjoys working together in this group because of the united leadership.

ABC Creation

There is this other group where I am a member. Actually, the others have blamed me for its creation. As a member of a Toastmasters club, one of the leadership challenges I had to work through was assisting another club that had low membership. One of our first discussions was about the goals of their club. I found that they intended to develop the skills to become professional speakers. While the club was focused on speaking and leadership, there was no guidance to become a professional speaker.

One of our friends, who is a professional speaker, advised us that we would need material to sell to attendees before we could be professional. We looked at each other and decided that not one of us was up to writing our own book. I suggested that we work together and write about a common topic. It took a bit of discussion as I convinced them that writing a book would have to occur outside of the current club for legal reasons. Yes, I take the blame for the creation of the Alternative Book Club, affectionately known as ABC.

I do not consider myself the leader and yet, I have led by giving directions. I have acted the part by getting the group to step up and use their varied talents to help create our products. Keith has done the legal duties to create the entity. If you have looked at our books, you will note that the editor role changes each time.

It is a reminder that we are in this together and are helping each other along the path of creating books. We have found that each of us has different abilities that come together to lead us toward our goal of creating books. (Check out our list of products at the end of this book!)

Enough time has passed that I am not sure any of us wants to go professional as a speaker, yet, we are not opposed to it if given the opportunity!

It has been fun to watch those who think they are not leading propel others in the group. As we review each other's chapters, writers are challenged by "readers" as to how we can better express our thoughts to give you a worthy product. Peers can be leaders from within a group! Peers in our group ask questions of the writers when a better example may be needed to clarify our point or someone needs to rewrite using complete sentences.

Is a hierarchy necessary?

While you may be familiar with "the boss" being the leader, did you give thought to a parent being a leader? Have you been in situations where your peers took turns with each other to lead projects? Have you worked under a controlling leader? Have you worked in an environment where leadership was lacking?

Without some form of hierarchy, it is difficult to have people work toward a common goal. While the amount of hierarchy can range from a subtle group of peers working together to make quilts or write books to that micromanager who wants nothing to do with a female in the workplace, we need leadership. When it comes down to the bottom line, we have been led since we were born. Whether we saw our parents as leaders or not, they set the example for us to follow.

As we become adults, we assume leadership roles whether we realize it or not. We become parts of the hierarchy ourselves. Whether or not we see ourselves as leaders, we are. The challenge comes in how we lead others. Our personal decisions are just that: personal decisions. They are what lead us through life. They give us the experiences we need.

Whether we are in an office environment or at home, we are leading. Who? Me? A leader? Yes! As the quote at the beginning of this chapter says, *"The hardest person you will ever have to lead is yourself."* Thank you, Bill George, for that honest quote. Thus, the most important leadership role we can have, is how we lead ourselves.

Conclusion

When you sit down and think about it, while we think of a leader as one directing others, what we need to focus on is how we lead ourselves. If we are considerate about our personal needs, we will be a better leader by being considerate of those we lead.

Reflection Questions

1. What qualities did you like in your favorite boss?

2. What qualities were the most troubling in a boss?

3. What were the favorite qualities displayed by your parent(s)?

4. What parental qualities were the hardest to live with?

5. How have you developed your leadership skills? Watch and learn? Professional development? Membership in a leadership organization?

6. What skills do you feel you need to improve personally?

7. What are your best leadership skills? How do you demonstrate them?

7

Leadership Will Find You

By: Keith Jones

"My definition of leadership is simple: Leader: anyone who influences someone. That means parents, teachers, employees, entrepreneurs, and even friends-all of us have the capacity to lead. Whether we realize it or not, we are already influencing others. The real question is: Are we being intentional about the influence we have?"

~Ryan Avery

Learning about Leadership

In this book, you have been learning about leadership. You have read about how keeping notes of each leadership situation will help you to be a better leader. To be the best leader you can be starts with modeling the behavior you want to see in others. In Randy's experience in the military, you have read about how leadership comes naturally to some people and not to others. We also have discovered that leadership usually takes two forms: formal (through either an elected or appointed position) and informal (where someone not in a formal position exerts leadership through experience, expertise or force of personality). It comes down to the fact we need leaders and followers. Leaders benefit from keeping an open mind and listening to their followers. In these situations, we are not alone when we doubt our leadership abilities.

In the previous chapters, I think each of those authors would agree with Ryan Avery's definition of a leader. A leader is anyone who influences someone. His question is, *"Are we being intentional about the influence we have?"*

There are times when we do not intend to become a leader. But somehow, when we least expect it, leadership has a way of walking up to us, taking us by the hand, and saying, "Now you will become a leader." At first, you will not see your full capacity to lead. Your challenge will be to be intentional about the influence you have. This experience will change not only your life but the lives of those you will lead.

Even When Not Looking, Leadership Will Find You.

When you least expect it, there are times when leadership confronts you in a way you do not expect. My wife and I were attending the parent's orientation for my son's grade school. He had finished kindergarten last school year and now was entering first grade.

My son took my hand and dragged me down the hallway. "Come with me Dad, I've got something to show you!" My son was pulling me with all his might. I was evidently not moving fast enough for him. I could tell this must be something very important to him. Down the main hallway, around the corner, we stopped halfway down this narrow corridor in front of a plaque hanging on the wall. "Dad, I want my name on that plaque." I asked him, "Son, do you know what that plaque is for?" "Yeah, Dad, I want to join Cub Scouts!" "Son, this plaque of names are all the boys who attended this grade school who earned their Eagle Scout award." "Yeah, Dad, but I have to join Cub Scouts first. Some guy in a uniform came to class today and told us all about it"

And so, the journey started. I had some idea what I was signing up for. I had been a Cub Scout growing up. I had earned my Wolf, Bear, and Lion badges when I was in grade school. My first thought was excitement about going camping again. Growing up, my dad took us camping every summer as his way of getting away from work. I was about to learn how different it would be as the parent of a Cub Scout.

Our first Cub Scout Pack meeting was an eye-opener! Picture this, a gymnasium full of kids running around, screaming and yelling. The parents sitting at the back of the gym having their own conversations, ignoring their kids because someone else was supposedly keeping track of them. The Cub Master had a bullhorn trying to communicate by talking louder than the noise generated by all the chaos. There did not seem to be any organization to the meeting at all. This was no way to run a meeting.

Fast forward two years. The pack had a new Cub Master by then and the meetings were running a little smoother. My wife and I had volunteered to be den parents for the five boys in my son's den. We helped the boys earn their belt loops, arrow points, and badges.

At the meeting in March, the Committee Chair followed us out to the car after the Pack Meeting and asked "Keith, would you be our next Cub Master?" Here was leadership looking for me to step up. I said, "Sure I think I can be the Cub Master next fall."

"No, Keith, I think you misunderstood me." He said with a sense of urgency in his voice. "We need you to step up and be the Cub Master now. You see, our current Cub Master has been relocated out of town with his job and we need you to run next month's

Pack meeting. We will be having a committee meeting next week and would like you to attend. Would you be interested?"

I looked at my wife. She has always been there to support me. "How about I attend the Committee meeting and we talk more about my being the new Cub Master?" The Committee Chair agreed. I was not sure what I had just agreed to, but leadership had found me.

Leading a group of 30 elementary boys is very different from leading adults in a company work environment. The first couple of meetings as Cub Master were a little rough. As the leader, you need to keep the attention of six- through ten-year-old boys long enough to give them information about the pack. After racking my brain as to what to do, my wife suggested I do something different to keep the boys' attention. I came up with a plan. I showed up at the next pack meeting with a tennis ball. Just before the meeting, I gathered all the boys around me so their parents could not hear what I was saying. I told the boys we were going to have some fun. They had to keep their eyes on me. When I held the tennis ball in my hand, they had to be quiet. But, when I tossed it in the air, they could yell and scream as loud as they wanted to.

Everything was set. We all said the pledge of allegiance to the flag and settled in for the meeting. The boys were watching very intently. I could tell they were excited. I talked to them about when the pinewood derby was going to be and that they needed to get their dads to help them build their cars. The parents at the back of the room were starting to get loud in their own conversations. I tossed the ball in the air and the boys cut loose with a hoot and a holler. The parents froze. They looked at the boys who were now very quiet, with their eyes on me. The parents had not seen what I had done and the ball was back in my hand before they turned around.

I went on with my explanation about popcorn sales as if nothing had happened. The parents started up their conversations again and started to get louder. I again tossed the ball in the air and the boys filled the gym with screams. The parents froze again. This time one of the eight-year-olds said out loud "Don't you get it? Parents need to be quiet!" Not only did I have the boy's attention, but now I had the parents' attention.

Before I was Cub Master, the boys didn't have that many activities during the pack meetings. I gathered all the Den leaders together and asked them to get the boys in their dens to learn skits. Each Den would perform a skit at the pack meetings. This gave each den the opportunity to perform in front of the whole group. We even took carpet samples, flipped them upside down so as not to scratch the floor, and raced down the gym floor in relays. All of this new activity resulted in not only engaging the boys but also their parents. The Den leaders were excited about attending the Pack meetings. Everyone was having fun.

Besides the Pine Wood Derby, we set up and ran a Space Derby. The scouts built balsa wood rockets propelled by a rubber band and propeller. With eight parallel lines strung up across the gym, the boys wound the propellers and the rockets flew down the strings.

During the years I was Cub Master, I honed my leadership skills empowering the Den leaders to think outside the box to encourage the boys to earn more awards and sell more popcorn. That, in turn, benefited the troop by allowing the Pack to grow and engage more boys into the program. It was a lot of fun. Years later, I would have some of the boys from that pack come up to me and say how much fun they remember having at those pack meetings.

- A good leader will understand it's important to listen to your kids. They may have dreams you never thought of and need your help to accomplish them.

- A good leader will be aware of any doors that may open before you. It could be an opportunity to become a leader.

- Being a good leader means you need to keep the attention of those you are leading. To do so may require you to be creative.

- A good leader will always look for new ways to teach kids and people to have fun.

Wood Badge Training

My son was in his last year of Cub Scouts and in the following spring, he would cross over into Boy Scouts. I was approached by Steve; he was a parent of a boy who had crossed over to Boy Scouts the previous year. Steve said I should go to Wood Badge.

I asked him, "What is Wood Badge?" His response was, "You need to go." "Ok, what am I going to learn at Wood Badge?" I was a bit confused. Steve handed me the signup sheet and said," Trust me, you will have fun and learn a lot."

What is Wood Badge? Wood Badge is an advanced, national leadership course open only to Scouting volunteers and professionals. Participants are Scouters from Cub Scouting, Scouts BSA, Venturing, Sea Scouts, and Explorers, and district and council Scouters.

In preparation for the course, I was told to prepare to camp in platform tents for three days. There was a week between sessions and then back to the camp for another three days of camping and coursework. The course was held at the Boy Scout camp. Before going to camp, I inquired among my friends who had been to Wood Badge, "What was the course was like?" My inquiries were met with "Keith, you will do fine." But really, I received no information on the course.

From the time I arrived a camp on a Thursday evening until late Sunday night every presentation, every activity and every event was planned almost to the minute. Upon arrival, we were divided into patrols of six scouters. Gayle was our troop guide. She would make presentations, help us through our activities and basically point us in the right direction.

To say that Wood Badge is an immersive experience is totally true. I had always worn the adult leader's uniform shirt, but not always the complete uniform. I mean the shirt, the pants, the socks, the hat, and the patches properly placed on the uniform. I felt uncomfortable at first. That feeling passed very quickly when I realized everyone else was also in a complete uniform. By the end of the course, I was more than comfortable, I was proud to wear the scout uniform.

While wearing the uniform didn't inherently prove my leadership, it served as a visual symbol of commitment and dedication to Scouting, and was a way for me to show pride in the organization and its values, setting an example for Scouts and other leaders.

- A good leader always has their eyes open to opportunities for further education, especially when dealing with leadership.

Living the Values

The very first presentation was on living the values of scouting. Wood Badge is as much about the journey as the destination. Experiencing the highs and lows of the time with my patrol was vital to the process of learning. The foundation of scouting can be seen in the elements of values, vision and mission.

I have struggled with the thought of what my values are. Values are those core beliefs or desires that guide or motivate our attitudes and our actions. For me, I kept feeling I could not define my values. It took a long time before I realized my values were right before me in the Scout law. A scout is trustworthy, loyal, helpful, friendly, courteous, kind, obedient, cheerful, thrifty, brave, clean, and reverent.

- As a good leader, you should understand your values, and living them will affect both you and those around you.

A vision states the goals a leader wants to achieve. They need to be able to see where they want themselves, their family, and their unit to be in the future. A vision is a picture of future success. As the cub master at the time, my vision was to bring more information to the cub scout pack through a pack newsletter. This would contain information so the parents and the scouts could plan their activities with more information about meeting times and events.

- A good leader needs to share their vision so everyone will understand what success looks like.

A mission is the purpose of the organization--why the organization exists. A leader who defines the purpose of the organization, sets the long-term objectives to align with its core values. The mission statement for scouts is to prepare young people to be responsible citizens and leaders who make ethical choices. My mission for attending Wood Badge was to experience and learn the leadership skills needed to be a better leader in scouting. Little did I know at the time all of the adventures this would lead me to in the future.

- A good leader defines their mission to clearly understand the purpose of their group or organization.

Listening to Learn

I don't think any of us fully appreciate the skill of listening. We do it all the time, but almost always we are listening only to the level of waiting for the time we can interject our opinions on whatever topic is being discussed. Yes, listening is a skill. It's no surprise that after defining the value of this training, the next topic was listening.

In the six days of Wood Badge, as participants, we were going to be immersed in so much information, presentations, and experience, so it was of utmost importance that we understood the power of listening. Listening is such a large part of being intentional about the influence we wield as leaders.

Effective communication is broken down into two parts, active and empathetic. Active listening reflects what a person is saying to confirm comprehension. By rephrasing the message and bouncing it back to the speaker, the listener confirms that the information has been properly received. Empathetic listening goes further. The listener is required to put themselves in the speaker's shoes and imagine things from the speaker's viewpoint, in other words, to understand how the speaker feels.

After the presentation on listening, we were given the opportunity to role-play to see if we understood what we were taught. Chuck and I were paired up. Our Troop Guide, Gayle, gave Chuck a piece of paper that I assumed told him which method of effective listening he was to use. I was to introduce myself to Chuck.

"My name is Keith. I have a son in Cub Scouts."

Chuck interrupted me with "Are we done here yet? I'm hungry, when do we eat?"

I was stunned. That isn't what was supposed to happen. Chuck wasn't using active or empathetic listening. I pressed on. "My wife and I are also Den Leaders."

"Can we get some snacks over here?"

I lost it. "That's not how this was supposed to work!"

Gayle stepped in. "No, Chuck was supposed to interrupt you. How do you handle a situation where someone is not listening to you?"

It was then I realized I was being tested on how well I handle situations. It was now apparent that the Wood Badge training was much more complicated than I originally thought. Every activity and every presentation were designed to test our reactions and help develop our leadership skills. How would I handle someone not listening to me? First, I needed to try to understand Chuck's perspective. I thought I was to be talking when I actually should have been communicating. I should have been using empathetic listening with Chuck to show I was engaged, using I statements to avoid defensiveness.

Chuck chuckled, "Sorry about that. I was doing what I was told to do on this paper. By the way are there any snacks around?"

- A good leader knows how powerful the act of active, engaged, empathetic listening is to be a better communicator.

Giving and Receiving Feedback

Receiving feedback can sometimes be difficult. However, by using effective listening skills, a feedback situation may be turned into a positive experience.

All of the other authors in this book are members of an organization known as Toastmasters International. In Toastmasters members learn to give evaluations as feedback.

The evaluation goes something like this. What did you excel at? What can you improve on? And what do you do to challenge yourself next time?

Anyone can give positive, superficial feedback. Comments like "Good job today." Are nice to say, but aren't very helpful. Understanding feedback helps define how to give it properly.

In a scouting or even a work situation:

- Deal only with the behavior that can be changed.
- Describe the behavior, don't evaluate it.
- Let the other person know the impact the behavior has on you.
- Use an "I" statement to accept responsibility for your own perceptions and emotions.
- Ask the other person to rephrase what they heard you say. That will ensure they understand your message.
- Show you care.

As an example after Wood Badge training, I was on a campout with the troop in South Dakota. It was close to lunchtime and most of the scouts were still working on their merit badges. Shawn had finished early and was about to prepare lunch. Shawn was going to light the propane stove. He turned the propane tank on first. Then proceeded to turn on the gas on the stove before lighting a match. Let's stop right here. Proper procedure is to light the match first before ever turning the gas on the stove itself.

My first question to Shawn was to ask, "Shawn, what are you doing?"

Shawn's reply was "Lighting the stove to heat up lunch." The gas was on and Shawn was still trying to light the match.

"Shawn, don't we first light the match before we turn on the gas?" I picked up the chair I was sitting in and moved a little farther away from the stove. If Shawn actually got the match lit, I was afraid the whole area would go up in flames.

"Oh, no, Mr. Jones, we always turn on the gas before lighting the match." Shawn was still struggling to light the match.

Using the I statement, "I feel like we need to be safe, Shawn. Where do you think the gas is going without the match being lit? I think this gas-rich air might react unfavorably and I am not sure how much of the camp will still be standing! Please turn off the gas to the stove and let's see why you are having trouble lighting the match."

Shawn turned off the gas to the stove. We let the gas dissipate from the area before attempting to figure out the reason Shawn was having trouble with the match.

I could have yelled at Shawn about the whole situation. But I realized effective communication was more productive and safer than yelling.

- A good leader will always find a way through effective communication to give positive feedback.

Stages of Team Development

Anyone who has ever watched a reality show knows that grouping a bunch of people together and giving them a name doesn't make them an effective team. This was true with our Wood Badge patrol as it is in any work environment. To morph a collection of individuals into a cohesive group, we needed good leadership, willing teammates and ample time. We had good leadership. We were somewhat willing teammates. But we had very little time. The course offered a better firsthand lesson in effective team development than anything else out there. Wood Badge allowed Scouters to experience Baden Powell's vision (Baden Powell was the founder of Scouting) for a perfect, youth-led scout troop. Participants didn't just read about how scouting should be run; we ate, slept, and drank it for six full days.

Wood Badge patrols develop in four distinct stages. Take a look at these stages first introduced by psychologist Bruce Tuckman in 1965. Consider how they apply to both your work and scouting roles.

- **Forming:** Like a pile of pickup sticks, everyone's moving in several directions without any sense of where to go or who does what. Everyone is tentative and polite.
  - Major issues: personal well-being, acceptance, and trust

- **Storming:** The group is at odds with one another. Disagreements are common, and subgroups form that polarize the team. Communication breaks down.
  - Major issues: power, control, and conflict

- **Norming:** Issues from "Storming" are addressed and resolved, boosting morale. Technical skills increase, and there's more clarity, trust, and cohesion. Team members start saying "we" more than "I."

- Major issues: sharing of control and
  avoidance of conflict

- **Performing:** Productivity and morale are high.
  Purpose, roles, and goals are clear. Mutual respect
  and trust abound.
  - Major issues: continued refinements and
    growth

Take a look at each one of these stages. How many of us have been in a new job, put into a new group, or a new position and realized we are struggling with just stage one? We often get past the intro stage and then we are stuck in stage two, storming, and can never seem to get to the next stage. We never can resolve or address issues from our storming stage. Only good leadership can get you to that final stage of performing.

The entire Wood Badge course is designed to be an obstacle course for your emotions. Every bump, U-turn and roadblock along the way is placed there intentionally by the creators of the course. What could be the purpose behind all of these obstacles? Each night I would lie in my tent totally exhausted, my mind a blur from the day's activities, wondering what kind of a sick, twisted person designed this crazy course.

As it turns out, the course designers weren't crazy. They were more like evil geniuses. They realized the group-strengthening power of forcing a team into an "us against the world" mentality. Throughout the course, staffers rushed us from task to task, intentionally creating the same kind of stress we often put on our Scouts.

In six days of training, our patrol experienced all of these stages. During the course, our patrol formed, stormed, normed, stormed, normed, performed, and stormed again. What I am saying is that every new opportunity is never faced with just the performing stage alone. There is going to be some conflict, some lack of communication, some new obstacles to overcome. In every situation, at work, at home, and in other organizations, you need to constantly learn new skills and trust others and their ideas. With any team, as with our patrol, we faced obstacles in our stages of development. This led us to change.

- A good leader understands the stages of team development, what stage his team is in, and how to lead them through each stage.

Leading Change

Change is inevitable. How do you face change? Do you run away from it? Do you resist it with all your might? Or do you lean into change and lead others through it?

At Wood Badge we learned how and why to accept change and lead others so that we controlled our response to change.

We experience change every day. Throughout our work, home, and lives, change is always happening.

There are six steps to leading a group through change:

- **Step 1 – Recognize that change happens.**

  It's inevitable. Once you can accept that "different" doesn't always mean "worse," you're on the right track. The more quickly that realization happens, the easier it is to accept the challenges the future presents. Eventually, you'll learn to savor the new opportunities.

  At Wood Badge change happened hourly. In the first few hours alone, I was ushered from one activity to the next without any agenda or guidance as to what was happening next. I complained we were not being told what was happening. The response was. "How do you handle your Cub Scouts? Do you tell them upfront what is going on at your Pack meetings?" Got me there! I see I need to make a change at our meetings.

165

- **Step 2 - Empower others to help you lead change.**

  You've got friends in life and in Scouting. Learn how to rely on and support each other. Just as a politician surrounds themself with trusted advisers, you should find a close contingent of people with the willingness, expertise, leadership prowess, and credibility to help you enact change.

  At Wood Badge this happened naturally. Wood Badgers are a self-selecting bunch. The only people who bother paying for this course in time and money are the most dedicated volunteers. (Nobody else is crazy enough to try!) In my patrol, I was the clear rookie, meaning I had plenty of opportunities to learn from others' experiences. As the days passed, we found common ground and grew stronger as a team.

- **Step 3 - Lead change based on values, vision, and mission.**

  If we don't know where we're going, how will we get there? To lead change, we need to know where we're headed. This means understanding our values (the Scout Oath and Law), our vision (the desired end result), and our mission (the steps necessary to get there).

At Wood Badge, I learned the real purpose of values, vision, and mission. Each of these can help define the core beliefs, the goals, and the purpose of the organization or business, and even your life.

- **Step 4—Establish urgency.**

People need a compelling reason to change. Without urgency, great ideas sit idle for months or years. This makes Scout units stagnant and gives Scouts a reason to drop out. To create urgency, show others the vision of what change can do, and outline the steps needed to make that change possible, necessary, and desirable.

At Wood Badge, urgency *was in every part of the course.* The course was designed to put our patrol through the fire as a group. When we came out on the other side, we were all stronger because of it.

- **Step 5—Move ahead, regardless.**

You're going to encounter some sticks-in-the-mud along the way--people unwilling to accept the inevitability of change. Your approach, to paraphrase Dori in *Finding Nemo*, is to "keep swimming." Bring these Scouters along for the ride (but let them sit in the back seat at first). As change occurs, they might come around and get pumped. If the lightbulb stays off for them, they'll eventually remove themselves. Call it survival of the fittest.

At Wood Badge, fortunately, there were no sticks in the Wood Badge mud. But each of us had moments of crankiness and reluctance where we dragged our heels a bit. Thankfully, everyone stayed pointed toward the goal, threw our arms around the stragglers, and moved forward.

- **Step 6—Create a culture that embraces change.**
  Whether we're talking about a small team of people, a Scouting unit, a business, or an entire organization, it's important to actively seek out change. Those who stand still get left behind. So, in your pack, troop, team, ship, post, or crew, make sure you're seeking out ideas. Remember, there are no bad ideas. Nothing stifles innovation faster than a brainstorming session where participants feel uncomfortable.

At Wood Badge, because we had just six days, this applies less to the actual course than to the aftermath. Each Scout leader experienced these steps firsthand and left with the tools to bring home. Now they had a chance to create that change culture in their own unit.

There is a reason they update the dictionary every year to add new words. The world is constantly changing. That's why lifelong learning is such an important concept, and it is the best way to embrace change at a personal level. I always told my kids, "You are either the teacher or the student and sometimes both. No matter the situation, a good leader always looks for the opportunity to teach other people what you know, or learn from their knowledge on a subject."

- A good leader recognizes change and is not afraid to lead through it.

Leaving a Legacy

How do you describe an event that has had such an impact on your life? This course taught me the skills and understanding to lead a successful pack and troop and build a successful relationship between the youth and adults. To this day, this was the most intense six full days of training I have ever experienced.

When I arrived home after that first weekend, I was exhausted. It was a physically and mentally draining experience. On the physical side, this was the summer my son wanted to go to every Cub Scout camp possible. Besides the Wood Badge weekend camps, I was in a tent on the weekends for six weeks straight. Mentally, I was transitioning from an adult-led cub scout pack to a boy-led troop. Wood Badge was teaching me how to make that transition.

Participating in this course gave me a deeper understanding of the what and why of scouting. The experience of learning the training material and doing the activities will stay with me my whole life. The course was even fun and I made some lifelong friends. To build stronger units in scouting, the leaders need this kind of training.

- A good leader will always be making transitions to the next step in their leadership journey.

What's in This for You?

The following is a summary of all the "good leader" statements in this chapter. I hope you can learn from them a few things about being a good leader. Always be aware of leadership training wherever possible. No matter your age you can always learn something more.

Even When Not Looking, Leadership Will Find You.

- A good leader will understand it's important to listen to your kids. They may have dreams you never thought of and need your help to accomplish them.

- A good leader will be aware of any doors that may open before you. It could be an opportunity to become a leader.

- Being a good leader means you need to keep the attention of those you are leading. To do so may require you to be creative.

- A good leader will always look for new ways to teach kids and people to have fun.

Wood Badge Training

- A good leader always has their eyes open to opportunities for further education, especially when dealing with leadership.

Living the Values

- As a good leader, you should understand your values, and living them will affect both you and those around you.

- A good leader needs to share their vision so everyone will understand what success looks like.

- A good leader defines their mission to clearly understand the purpose of their group or organization.

Listening to Learn

- A good leader knows how powerful the act of active, engaged, empathetic listening is to be a better communicator.

Giving and Receiving Feedback

- A good leader will always find a way through effective communication to give positive feedback.

Stages of Team Development

- A good leader understands the stages of team development, what stage his team is in, and how to lead them through each stage.

Leading Change

- A good leader recognizes change and is not afraid to lead through it.

Leaving a Legacy

- A good leader will always be making transitions to the next step in their leadership journey.

<u>Chapter Wrap-up</u>

I enjoyed writing this chapter. By reviewing the training I received through Wood Badge, I did not realize how much I had forgotten about leadership. I promise I will spend more time with my notes and my friends who made this training possible. They are the true leaders.

I would also like to thank Ryan Avery, World Champion of Public Speaking 2012, for letting me use his quote on leadership. As a speaker who travels the world, he truly is very intentional about the influence he has in people's lives. Thank you, Ryan!!!

After reading this chapter, after reading this book, I challenge all readers to be aware that you are a leader because you influence others. I challenge all of you to be intentional about that influence.

Reflection Questions

1. What steps have led you to Leadership?

2. Has leadership found you in ways you did not expect? What are those ways?

3. Has this changed your perspective on Leadership?

4. What leadership training have you attended? Was it effective?

5. Write down your values.

6. Write down a vision just for yourself.

7. Write down a mission just for yourself.

8. How have you really thought about listening as a skill?

9. Practice active listening.

10. Practice empathetic listening.

11. Practice giving feedback in a positive way.

12. Are you a member of a team? Where is the team with respect to its stage of development?

13. Write down how you can relate to the six steps leading change.

14. Write down what kind of a legacy you would like to leave for people to remember.

Meet Our Authors

Janel Asche

Janel Asche is a contributing author for four previous books in the Spotlight on the Art series. She made her writing debut in Spotlight on the Art of Gratitude, then wrote again for Spotlight on the Art of Speaking and Spotlight on the Art of Confidence. Most recently she wrote for Spotlight on the Art of Story.

A long-time technical analyst, Miss Janel now leads much more interesting, much smaller people, occasionally engaging in games of "follow the leader" and "Simon says." She feeds her hunger for big-people leadership through Toastmasters where she is surrounded by a fascinating diversity of supportive friends and fellow members.

Ms. Asche has lived in Nebraska all her life and has been married more than two-thirds of that time. She has four grown children, two grown children-in-law, one granddaughter, and two grandsons.

Contact Janel at janel@alternativebookclub.com.

Mark Fegan

Mark Fegan is a 1975 graduate of Morningside College in Sioux City, Iowa. His primary area of study was Mathematics Education. After graduation Mr. Fegan began a teaching career that lasted twenty years. After starting his career as a Junior High teacher in Minnesota, he taught High School Mathematics and Computer Science in Nebraska and completed this phase of his life in 1996 as an Assistant Professor at Peru State College in Nebraska. Along the way, he took a one-year hiatus to work in the garment industry and an additional year off for graduate school. Mr. Fegan earned his Master of Science in Education from Kearney State College in Nebraska in 1979. In 1996, Mr. Fegan changed his focus from education to Software Developer for Raytheon.

Mr. Fegan joined Toastmasters International in October 2009 and earned Distinguished Toastmaster status in August 2014. Mr. Fegan continues to be active in Toastmasters where he has served as District Director, the highest elective district office, for Toastmasters District 24 in 2020 - 2021.

In line with his lifelong interest in education, Mr. Fegan has also led the Alternative Book Club's Writers Workshop project--a set of workshop modules to assist an aspiring writer become a published author. This work is ongoing.

Mr. Fegan lives with his wife Rebecca in Bellevue, Nebraska, and continues to take an interest in education and helping others achieve their goals.

Contact Mark at: Mark@alternativebookclub.com

179

Rebecca Fegan

Rebecca Fegan is insatiably curious; she is a bibliophile and incessant researcher. Having worked many jobs throughout her life, she has gotten experience in quite a few fields and finds it fascinating to see correlations. In addition to her Music Education degree, she also picked up a degree in Business administration and is a Financial Analyst focusing on Investments. She is also an Accredited Coach by the European Mentoring and Coaching Council as a Founding Member of the Conscious Coaching Academy.

She has used her coaching acumen with her 5 children, her 5 grandchildren, and the thousands of students she's taught in her nearly six-decade career.

Growing up in a musical family, she is drawn to culture--art, literature, music, religion, and history. As the owner and operator of the Fine Arts Academy, and a member of Primerica Financial Services, she is embarking on a third business, The Fegan Method of Learning where she helps people acquire the information and skills, they need to fulfill their dreams and destinies. She and Mark Fegan have been happily married since 1977.

As a member of Toastmasters, she has served in several capacities: District Administration Manager 2024-2025, District Club Retention Chair 2020-2023, District Treasurer, Division Director, and Area Governor. She currently belongs to three clubs. She really loves to compete!

Contact Rebecca at rebecca@alternativebookclub.com

Pamela Hughes

Pam Hughes is venturing into unfamiliar territory with this collaboration. She is a loving spouse and mother, loyal friend, dedicated employee, and helpful volunteer to many. And she is now adding co-author to her resume. She grew up in an Air Force family, spending her formative years traveling through Europe. She earned a Bachelor of Science in Business Administration with dual majors in Management and Accounting from the University of Nebraska at Omaha.

Pam has been fortunate to work for a regional bank and two Fortune 500 companies in Omaha. Her broad range of jobs include retirement plan administration, project management, and IT management. Now retired, she is immersing herself in golf and traveling Europe. A Toastmaster since 2008, she has enjoyed meeting with and serving constituents around Nebraska while holding several District leadership roles. She has been married for 37 years and raised two children who also live in Omaha.

Christine Jones

Christine Jones never felt that she was leadership material. As this book was evolving, she reflected on her work experiences. Focusing on leaders she has had led her to find moments when she experienced good and bad leaders. She also found times when she did lead.

She has been a wife of over 40 years to Keith Jones. She has two successful adults that she led to maturity. She is now the grandmother of two grandsons and one granddaughter. She savors the visits with these future leaders.

She is an active member of the speaking and leadership organization known as Toastmasters International. Learning to prepare and present speeches in front of a small group of people allows her to reflect on many life experiences. Like writing these chapters, many of her speeches are based on what she knows. Her family, her joy of quilting and cooking are frequent topics. As a member of a volunteer-led organization, she has been given opportunity to practice leadership skills as well as watch others lead and learn to be better leaders.

She is a founding member of The Alternative Book Club. Christine has been a regular contributor to the Spotlight on the Art of series produced by The Alternative Book Club.

Contact Mrs. Jones at christine@alternativebookclub.com.

Keith Jones

Keith Jones is the CEO, President and Founder of Kitewind LLC, a company formed to facilitate presentations, publishing, and consulting for individuals and corporations. He is a founding member of the Alternative Book Club.

During more than thirty years of being involved in the Toastmasters International organization, Keith refined his speaking skills resulting in several championships at the district level in Humorous, Tall Tales, and Evaluation contests. Keith has achieved the organizations highest designation of Distinguished Toastmaster (DTM). Keith has served as District Director for Toastmasters District 24 during the 2022-2023 year.

Keith has had the honor and privilege to be able to teach and instruct both youth and adults in the art of leadership. He has taught adults to successfully develop their leadership skills. Keith and his wife Christine are parents of two children and grandparents of three grandchildren. Keith is also a regular contributing author to the Spotlight on the Art of series of books published by the Alternative Book Club.

Contact Keith at Keith@alternativebookclub.com

Randy Prier

Randy Prier is a 22-year veteran of the US Air Force, having retired as a Lieutenant Colonel in 1993. During his time in the Air Force, he served in a variety of positions including Student Squadron Commander, Air Force Liaison with the Government of the US Territory of Guam, and Division Chief in the Headquarters, Strategic Air Command. His postings included Clark Air Base in the Philippines; Andersen AFB, Guam; Washington, D.C.; and Offutt AFB, Nebraska. Randy's military decorations include the Defense Meritorious Service Medal, the Meritorious Service Medal with three Oak Leaf Clusters, the Air Force Commendation Medal, and the Air Force Achievement Medal. Randy graduated from the University of Nebraska with a B.A. in Political Science in 1968 and earned a Master of Arts degree in International Affairs from the Catholic University of America in 1982.

As a member of Toastmasters International since 1981, Randy has earned the highest educational award of Distinguished Toastmaster three times and received the Toastmasters International Presidential Citation in 2006. He served as District Governor of Toastmasters District 24 (covering parts of Nebraska and Iowa) in 1992-3, earning the Distinguished District Award. From 2001-03, he served a two-year elected term on the Toastmasters International Board of Directors. As a frequent Toastmasters speech contest competitor, Randy has won District 24 championships in the International Speech, Humorous (twice), Evaluation and Table Topics contests. He has also been a runner-up in the District's Tall-Tale contest.
Randy and his wife, Kathy, have three grown children and five grandchildren. They live in Papillion, Nebraska, a suburb of Omaha.

189

Contact Randy at randy@alternativebookclub.com

More from the

Alternative Book Club

If you enjoyed this book, consider picking up a copy of our other books in the "Spotlight on the Art of "series

In *Spotlight on the Art of Grace*, you will be moved by powerful stories of personal loss and triumph. You will learn how to mend fences, how to make the world better, and all the while do it with energy and with a smile.

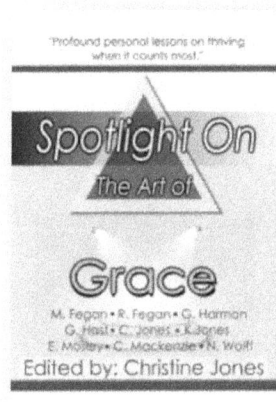

"Each Chapter offers lessons in Grace, with the contributing author sharing relevant stories with insight and thought-provoking discussion questions. I am impressed with the depth and diversity of perspectives into Grace, as the compilations include resiliency, perseverance, forgiveness, constructive feedback, principles-based leadership, collaboration and valuing others. Well-done! A must-read for anyone in leadership, management, or any type of relationship and wants to keep it healthy!"
- **Sheryl Roush, Speaker, 17-time Published Author**

Spotlight on the Art of Resilience

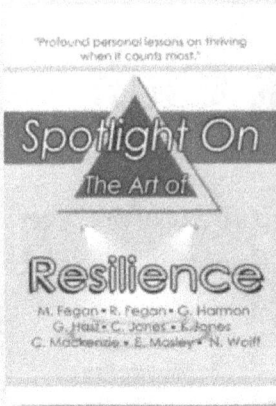

The by powerful stories of resilience will be a source of hope in hard times These are stories of getting through the challenges that are thrown at you. These may be jobs, relationships, or health.

Written by most of the same authors who wrote the previous titles, we hope these books will prove to be as beneficial to you as it was for us to write them.

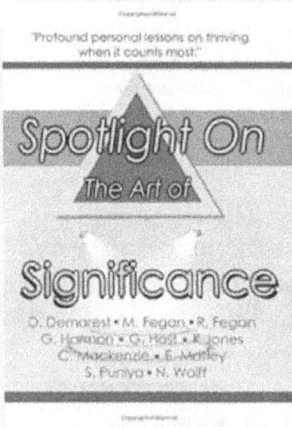

Spotlight on the Art of Significance

The stories in this book reveals the powerful impact we've had on each other. This impact at times might be hidden and gets revealed sometimes even years later. The stories in this book will help you realize the power and influence we often wield without ever knowing it.

Written by most of the same authors as in earlier Spotlight series books with some new faces, we hope this book will help you recognize significance in your own lives.

Spotlight on the Art of Fear

This seems unusual for a book title. How could there be an "Art" to fear? The stories covered in this book focus on the sources of our fears, how to face them and overcome them. Sometimes we must seek fearful situations in order for us to grow, to voluntarily go where we've never been before. The authors of this book have many unique perspectives that may strike a chord in your experiences. Read, absorb and apply this Art of Fear!

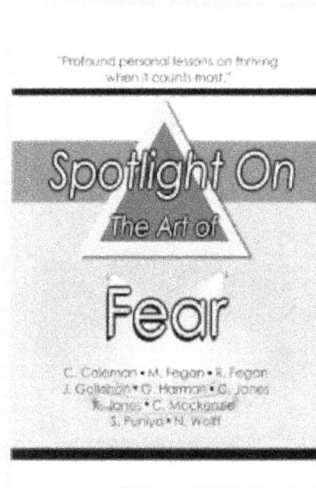

Spotlight on the Art of Generating Energy

Have you ever been in a room where the air crackled with excitement and creative thoughts? Do you know someone that brings positive energy to any situation? Have you ever wondered what makes some groups click and get monumental tasks done with ease? Our authors explore the energy-generating clues for the best results personally and in a group. Read this and charge yourself up!

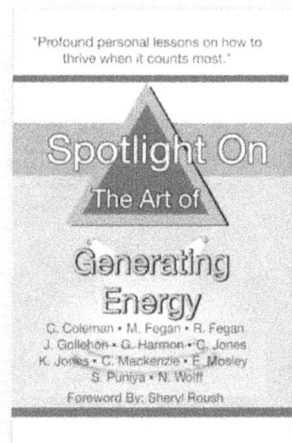

Spotlight on the Art of Gratitude

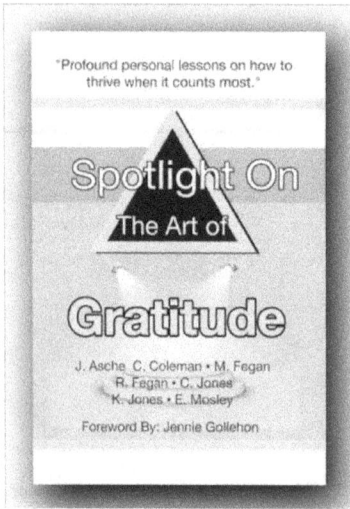

Do you have a mind and heart filled with gratitude? Are challenging times making it difficult for you to be grateful? How do you cope with times of isolation? How do you continue to feel gratitude in your life when facing challenges? This book provides answers to these and other questions.

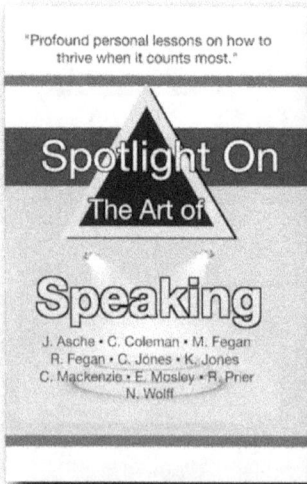

Spotlight on the Art of Speaking

Whether you are making a phone call or speaking to a group, we all speak. There may be times you struggle to find the words or you want to create a better speech. This compilation looks at many elements of how we speak. While many parts are serious, there is even room for humor.

Spotlight on the Art of Confidence
Confidence is an attitude that enables you to attempt new things during your life's journey. At times, you encounter situations that are new or challenging. Your confidence may falter or elude you. In this compilation, the authors share their insights on gaining, building and utilizing confidence.

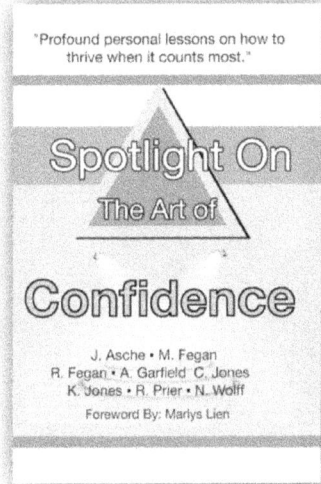

"Profound personal lessons on how to thrive when it counts most."

Spotlight On
The Art of

Confidence

J. Asche • M. Fegan
R. Fegan • A. Garfield C. Jones
K. Jones • R. Prier • N. Wolff

Foreword By: Marlys Lien

Spotlight on the Art of The Story
Stories capture our interest more easily than a dry recitation of facts. They bring to life experiences the teller wants to share, evoke empathy for the characters, and humanize the situations portrayed. In this compilation, the authors share their insights on how best to bring the stories within you to life.

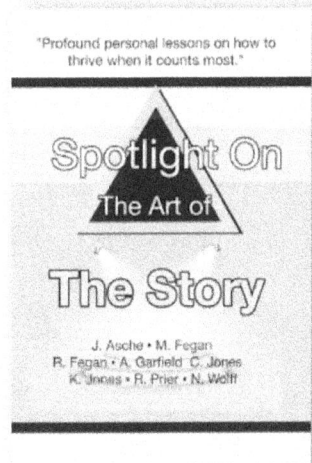

"Profound personal lessons on how to thrive when it counts most."

Spotlight On
The Art of

The Story

J. Asche • M. Fegan
R. Fegan • A. Garfield C. Jones
K. Jones • R. Prier • N. Wolff

Stay in touch with the Alternative Book Club as you continue to strive toward your goals, overcome adversity, and find your voice.

http://www.AlternativeBookClub.com

www.ingramcontent.com/pod-product-compliance
Lightning Source LLC
Chambersburg PA
CBHW031509270326
41930CB00006B/320

9 781966 649023